HASTINGS TRAMWAYS

Robert J Harley

Cover picture: The hub of the system was at the long-gone Memorial where very few minutes elapsed without a tram passing. Cars 62 and 55 run through Robertson Street after their journey along the seafront. The colours used on the cover of this book are similar to those used on Hasting trams.

First published August 1993

ISBN 1 873793 18 9

Design - Deborah Goodridge

Published by Middleton Press
Easebourne Lane
Midhurst
West Sussex
GU29 9AZ
Tel: (0730) 813169

Printed & bound by Biddles Ltd,
Guildford and Kings Lynn

CONTENTS

INTRODUCTION AND ACKNOWLEDGEMENTS

The main inspiration for this book came in several meetings with George Gundry whose history of the tramways in the area was published in Tramway Review in 1977. His enthusiasm is infectious, and he speaks with much affection of his favourite system with the long rides beating the bounds on the "circular" and the bracing trip along the front to Cooden Beach. He has devoted a life time preserving historic material on the Hastings Tramways and this album is a direct result of his scholarship. During my own childhood, holiday visits were often paid to Bexhill and Cooden; it always struck me that the trolleybuses which replaced the trams and lasted until 1959 had retained a lot of the tramway atmosphere. I became fascinated with the old style overhead and the vista of bracket arms stretching along Cooden Drive was a compelling invitation for further exploration. I must express my thanks to David C. Padgham who has supplied valuable views and tickets; his knowledge of local history has provided me with much important information. I also visited Derek Waters who was kind enough to share with me his collection of photographs and reminiscences of working at Silverhill depot on the trolley buses. Again I am grateful to C. Carter for his help on the photographic side. This book is dedicated to all these enthusiasts who have kept the memory of Hastings Tramways alive for so many years.

GEOGRAPHICAL SETTING

Hastings and the neighbouring seaside resorts of St.Leonards and Bexhill are situated on the south coast of England in the county of East Sussex. Inland from the Channel shore the ground rises steeply in places reaching heights of over 500 feet/150 metres above sea level. Old Hastings lies in a dip bounded by hills which stretch away from the coast to form the central Sandstone uplands of the Weald, a region of Southern England noted for its beautiful scenery.

A further dip in the hills occurs at Glyne Gap, where level fields stretch to the coast between Bexhill and St. Leonards at Pebsham Marshes. The western extemity of the system at Cooden was on the eastern boundary of the Pevensey Levels.

The maps are to the scale of 25" to 1 mile and are from the 1909 edition unless otherwise stated.

HISTORICAL BACKGROUND

The name of the town will always be associated with the events of 14th October 1066, when the current of British and world history was changed by the victory of Duke William of Normandy. The fight actually took place at Senlac some five miles inland from Hastings; the town which grew up at the location was aptly named Battle. After the Conquest, Hastings settled down as one of the Cinque Ports trading with the continent of Europe and it is noted that the town supplied around twenty ships to ward off the Spanish Armada which sailed up the Channel in 1588. The area was also well known for its contraband connections to the continent and in 1824 and 1828 fatalities occurred at Bexhill in fights between revenue men and smugglers. The arrival of railway links to the capital and along the coast, caused a growth in the town with much house building in the second half of

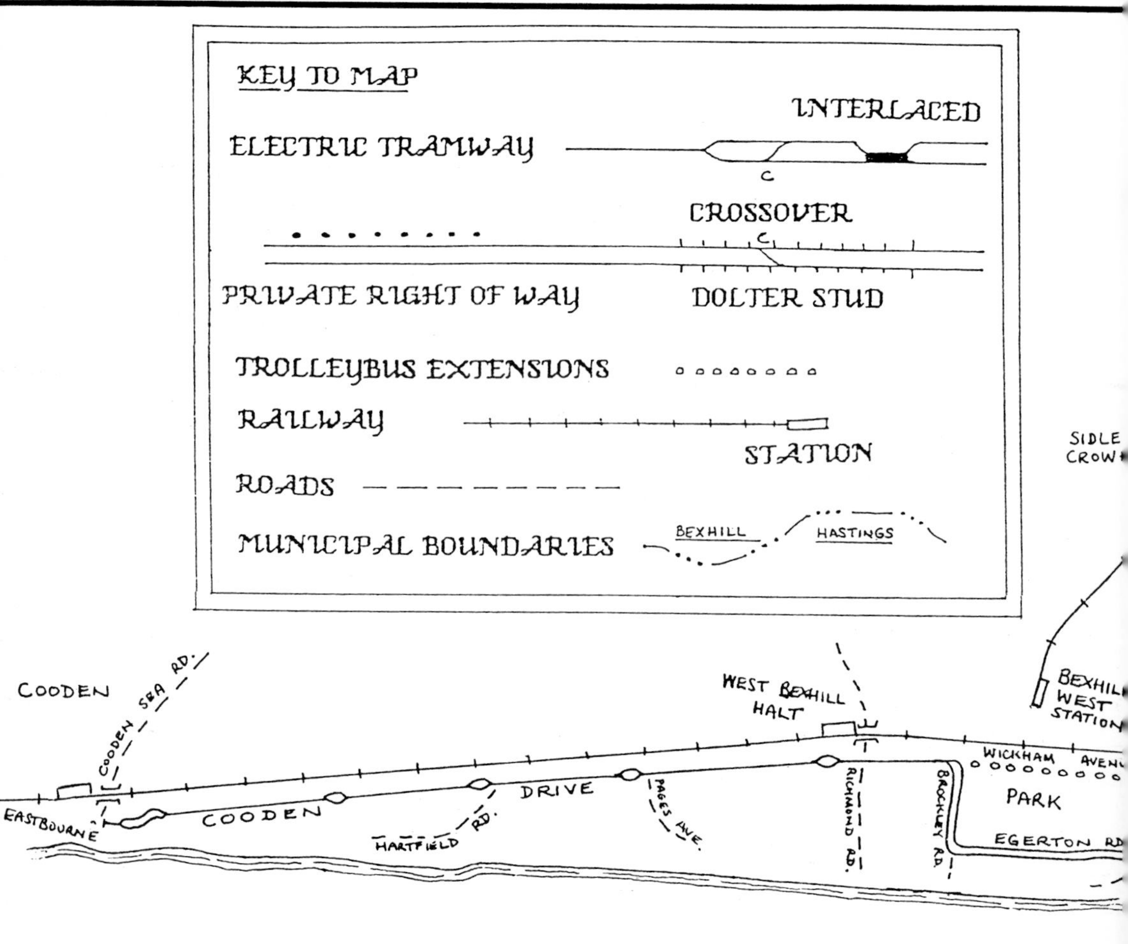

the nineteenth century. It became fashionable to "take the air" at St. Leonards and many fine residences were constructed to cater for an expected influx of well-to-do visitors; the quaintly named Decimus Burton was responsible for many of the buildings in St. Leonards. Away from the front, in the Old Town and some of the new suburbs, poverty was rife. These turn of the century social conditions have been graphically described by the literary son of Hastings, Robert Tressell.

Into this environment entered the Hastings Tramways Company; construction began in 1904 at the Harrow Inn, Baldslow, and the first tramcars arrived in July 1905. Public service commenced on 31st July 1905 on the circular route and a further line from Ore to the Market Cross, Old Town, opened in August. The proposed line along the front to St. Leonards, West Marina, was held up due to objections to overhead wires.

Another depot was constructed at Bulverhythe and services started between St. Leonards and Bexhill on 9th April 1906; finally the line reached the isolated outpost of Cooden on 28th July 1906. The Bexhill section included one length of private tramroad across Pebsham Marsh and a long straight run through cornfields on a newly constructed right of way from Egerton Park to Cooden Beach. The London Road extension from Silverhill to the seafront also opened in July.

On 12th January 1907 the connection between the two systems was made along the coast, with double track equipped with the Dolter stud contact system. This was the final extension; at its peak the system was just short of 20 route miles/32kms. Trams ran from the Memorial in Hastings to the Bopeep at St. Leonards trailing underneath them a 12ft./3.6 metres long skate which energised the studs to supply the traction current. In spite of problems with live studs, the Dolter line worked fairly well, but the Board of Trade instructed Hastings to replace it in 1913. The company then adopted petrol electric traction for the seafront; certain trams were fitted with petrol engines coupled to a dynamo which fed current to the controllers. The first petrol electric cars ran on 16th March 1914 and the last Dolter car on 26th March. The petrol electric experiment did not last long and the council admitted defeat and allowed overhead wires along the seafront; the new service started in March 1921.

In September 1926 service numbers were used for the following routes:

1 Silverhill - St. Leonards - Ore
2 Ore - High Street (Market Cross)
3 Bexhill - Ore
4 Hollington - Bohemia Road - Memorial
5 Ore - Bexhill
6 Cooden - St. Helens (Cemetery)
7 St. Helens - Cooden
8 Circular via Bohemia Road
9 Circular via St. Helens

Services 3, 5, 6 and 7 were unidirectional. In the mid-1920s the climate of opinion began

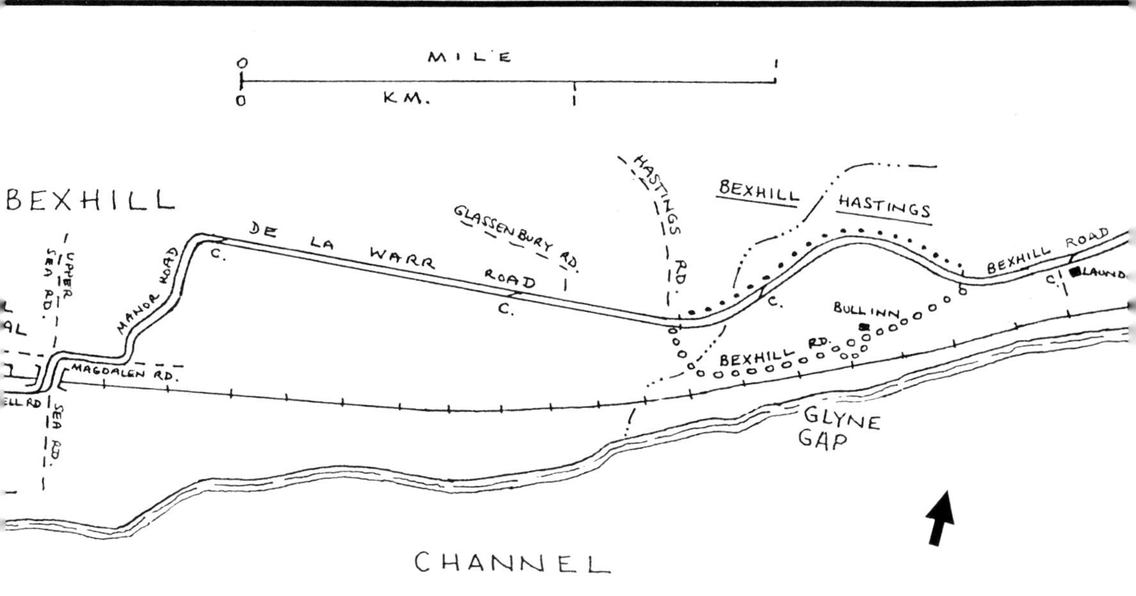

to change against the trams and various replacement options were mooted. As usual the two main councils involved, Bexhill and Hastings, could never quite see eye to eye concerning what form of transport should traverse their streets. Eventually all parties agreed on the substitution of trolleybuses for trams and the conversion began on 1st April 1928, with the last tram running on 13th March 1929. Thus ended the Hastings tramways, a comparatively early British tramway fatality. Most of the cars were sold off as sheds and at the time of writing (1993) car 43 is being kept at the Dover Transport Museum for restoration.

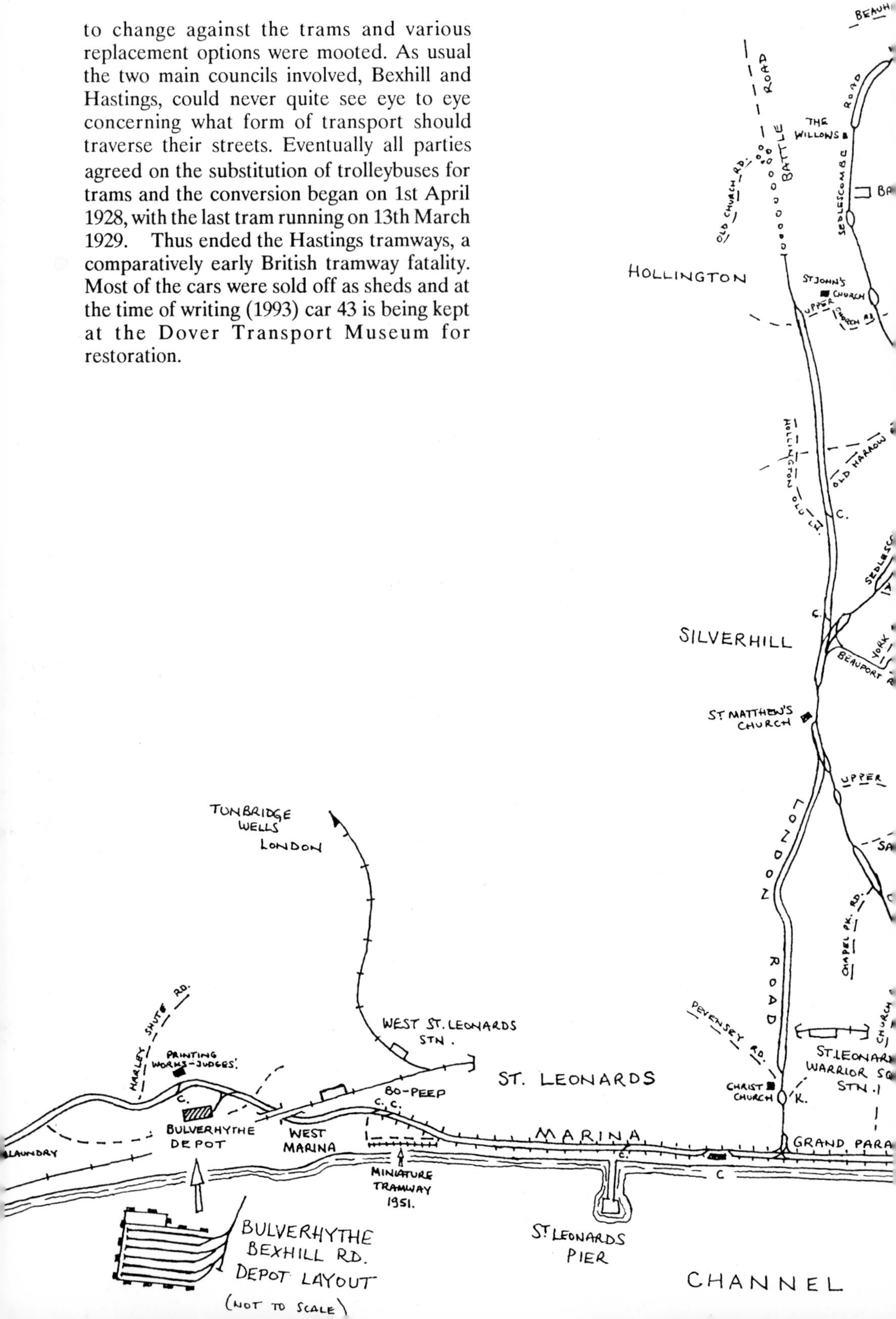

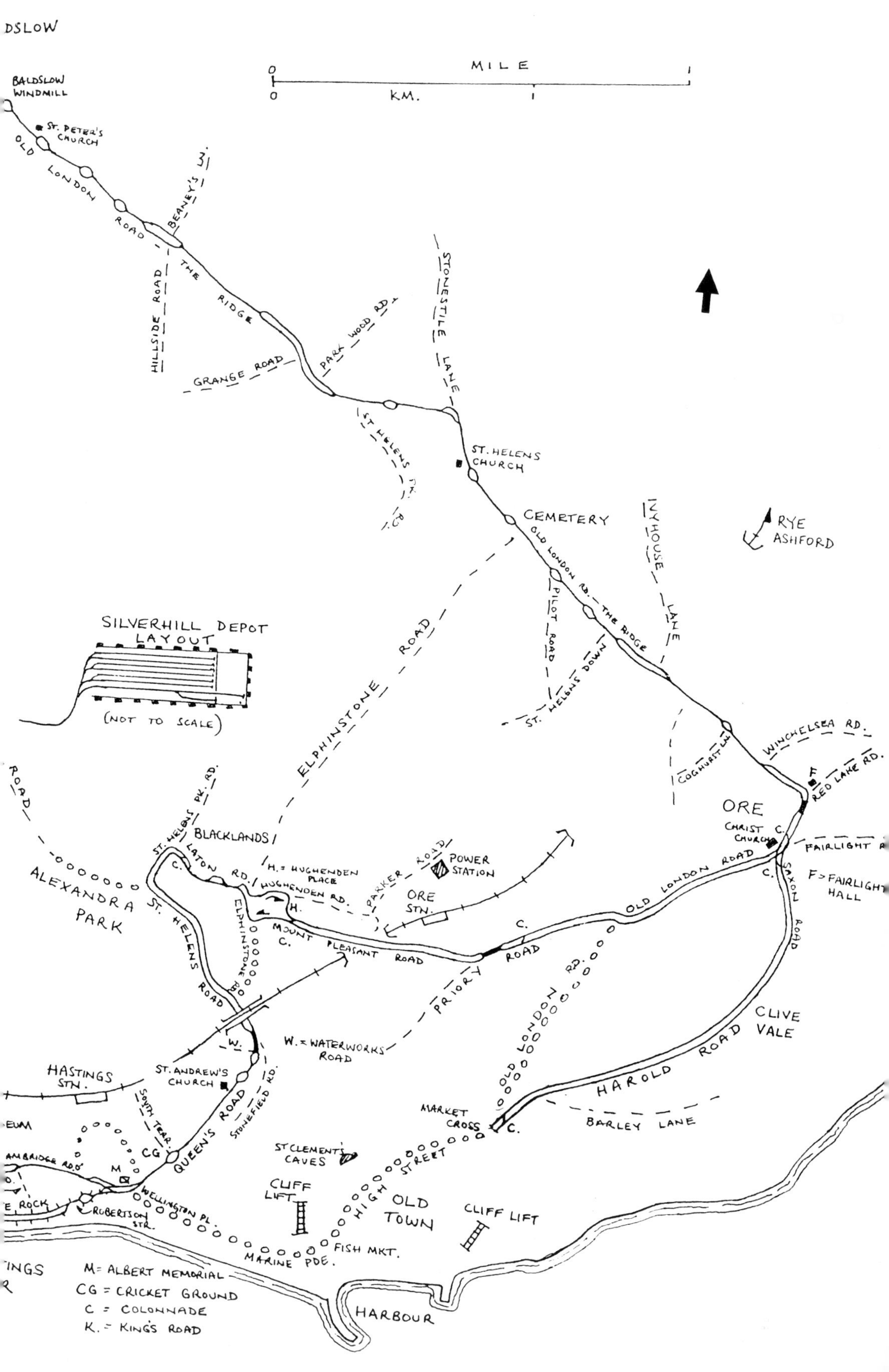

DSLOW
MILE
KM.
BALDSLOW WINDMILL
ST. PETER'S CHURCH
OLD LONDON ROAD
BEANEY'S
THE RIDGE
HILLSIDE ROAD
GRANGE ROAD
PARK WOOD RD.
STONESTILE LANE
ST HELENS PK. RD.
ST. HELENS CHURCH
CEMETERY
OLD LONDON RD. THE RIDGE
PILOT ROAD
IVYHOUSE LANE
RYE
ASHFORD
ST. HELENS DOWN
ELPHINSTONE ROAD
SILVERHILL DEPOT LAYOUT
(NOT TO SCALE)
COGHURST LN.
WINCHELSEA RD.
RED LAKE RD.
ORE
CHRIST CHURCH
FAIRLIGHT R
F = FAIRLIGHT HALL
SAXON ROAD
ROAD
ALEXANDRA PARK
ST. HELENS PK. RD.
BLACKLANDS
LATON RD.
ST. HELENS ROAD
H. = HUGHENDEN PLACE
HUGHENDEN RD.
PARKER ROAD
POWER STATION
ORE STN.
OLD LONDON ROAD
ELPHINSTONE RD.
MOUNT PLEASANT ROAD
PRIORY ROAD
OLD LONDON RD.
CLIVE VALE
HAROLD ROAD
W. = WATERWORKS ROAD
HASTINGS STN.
ST. ANDREW'S CHURCH
SOUTH TERR.
STONEFIELD RD.
QUEEN'S ROAD
MARKET CROSS
BARLEY LANE
EUM
AMBRIDGE RD.
CG
M
ST CLEMENTS CAVES
HIGH STREET
E ROCK
ROBERTSON STR.
WELLINGTON PL.
CLIFF LIFT
OLD TOWN
CLIFF LIFT
FISH MKT.
MARINE PDE.
TINGS
M = ALBERT MEMORIAL
CG = CRICKET GROUND
C = COLONNADE
K. = KING'S ROAD
HARBOUR

DOLTER STUD

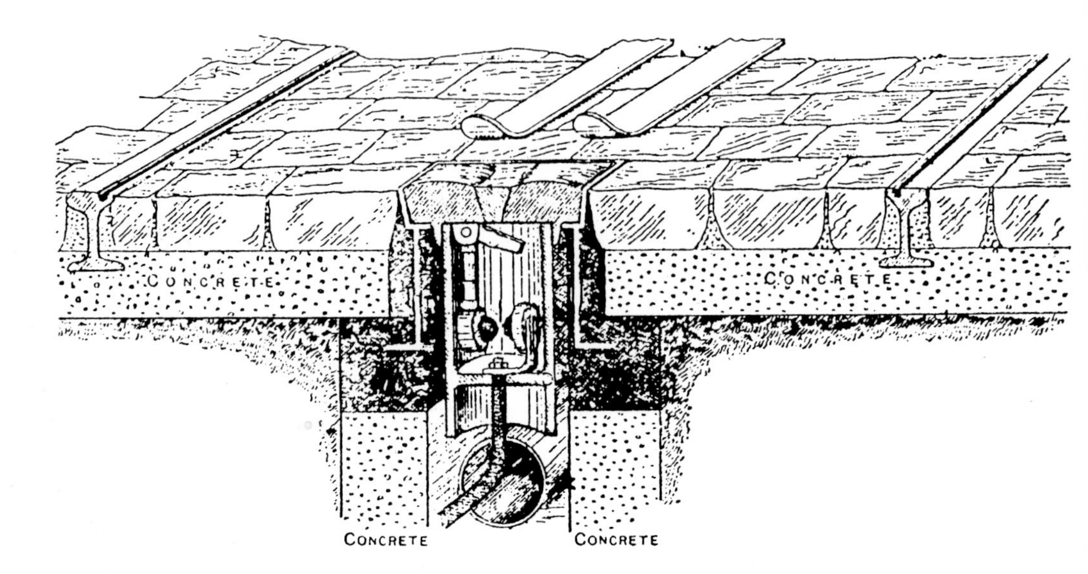

The Dolter Skate attached underneath the tram consisted of two metal skids. Here it approaches a "dead" stud - the circuit has not yet been made.

The magnetised skate passes over the stud causing the pivoted switch to move and close the circuit thus providing the traction current. After the skate has gone, the switch falls due to gravity and the circuit is broken.

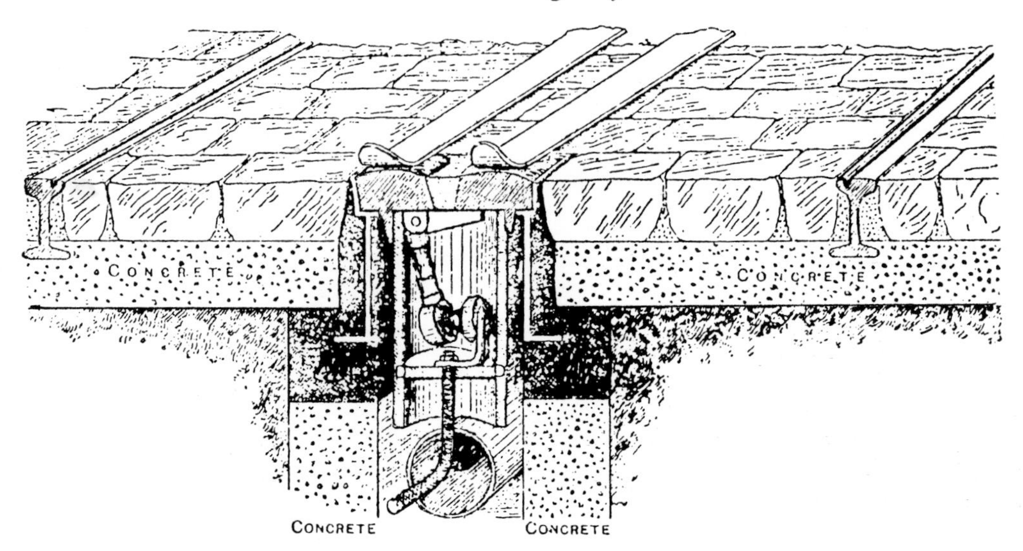

oss section of Dolter Stud and skate. The
ion current of 550 volts D.C. goes from the
: along the main power cable to the
ollers at either end of the tram. At
ngs, dual-fitted trams had a changeover
h operated by the motorman which was
ed Dolter Stud/Trolley. This was used at
Marina on through cars to Bexhill.

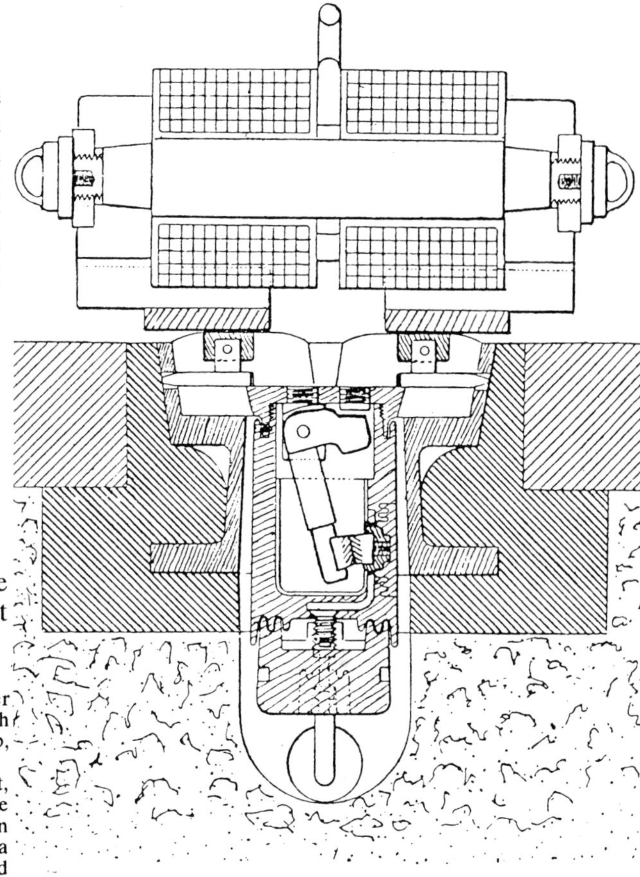

A contemporary account describes the
nod of operation of this unusual current
:ction system.

n Hastings, Torquay, and Mexborough the Dolter
:e-contact system is in use. The Dolter stud switch
, is fitted with a manganese-steel cover-plate b,
carrries two magnetic-steel pole pieces c.
nese pole pieces form part of the magnetic circuit,
anese steel being non-magnetic. Underneath the
-plate b is attached a gunmetal casting d, which in
upports a pot e, made of insulating material, and a
ng lever f hinged at g. Into the gunmetal casting d
ced two steel plugs h, which also form part of the
etic circuit. Carried by the lever f is a carbon contact
i, which, when the upper end of the lever is drawn
etically toward the plugs h, makes contact with a
carbon block j on the side of the pot. The contact
:ctrically connected, by means of the strip k, to the
; clips l, which fit over a tongue m coupled to the
cable n. The latter is laid in an earthenware trough
ch is then filled in with bitumen. In order to prevent
: from reaching the contacts l, m, the box
unding them is filled with heavy oil.
'he studs in the Dolter system are operated by a
et attached to the car, as in the Lorain system. As
agnet passes over each stud, the lever f, is attracted
ds, the carbon blocks i and j make contact, and the
nt passes from the cable n to the stud and then
gh the collecting skate to the controllers and
s. The studs are placed about 9 feet apart and the
is always in contact with one of them; when the car
ssd the stud, the lever f falls back by gravity to the
sition. As a safeguard against leaving live studs
d the car, a wire brush attached to the car
work makes contact with the stud after the magnet
ssed it; if the stud is alive, a fuse in the stud circuit
wn and the current is cut off.
e skate collector, carried on the car in the Dolter
n, consists of two long parallel bars hung low
h just to touch the studs. The skate bars are
etized with opposite polarity by three
omagnets placed between them. As the position of
rs is immediately over the pole pieces c, the magnet
is completed from the bars through the pole pieces
studs h, and the top portion of the rocking lever f.

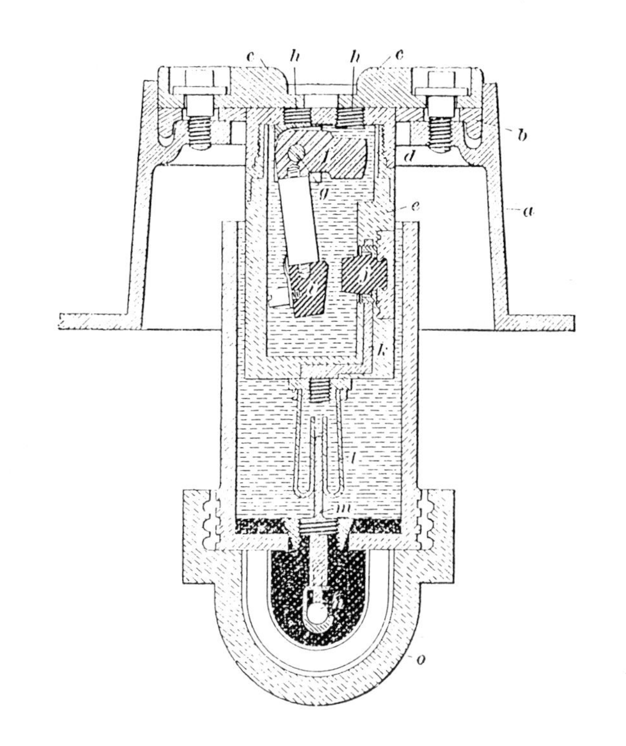

1. CIRCULAR SERVICE

1. Our journey over the Hastings tramways starts at the Albert Memorial in the town centre. The date is 15th July 1905 and car 10 is about to pull away on its first trial trip in front of a suitably impressed crowd waiting to see this wonder of mechanical transport. (G.L.Gundry Coll.)

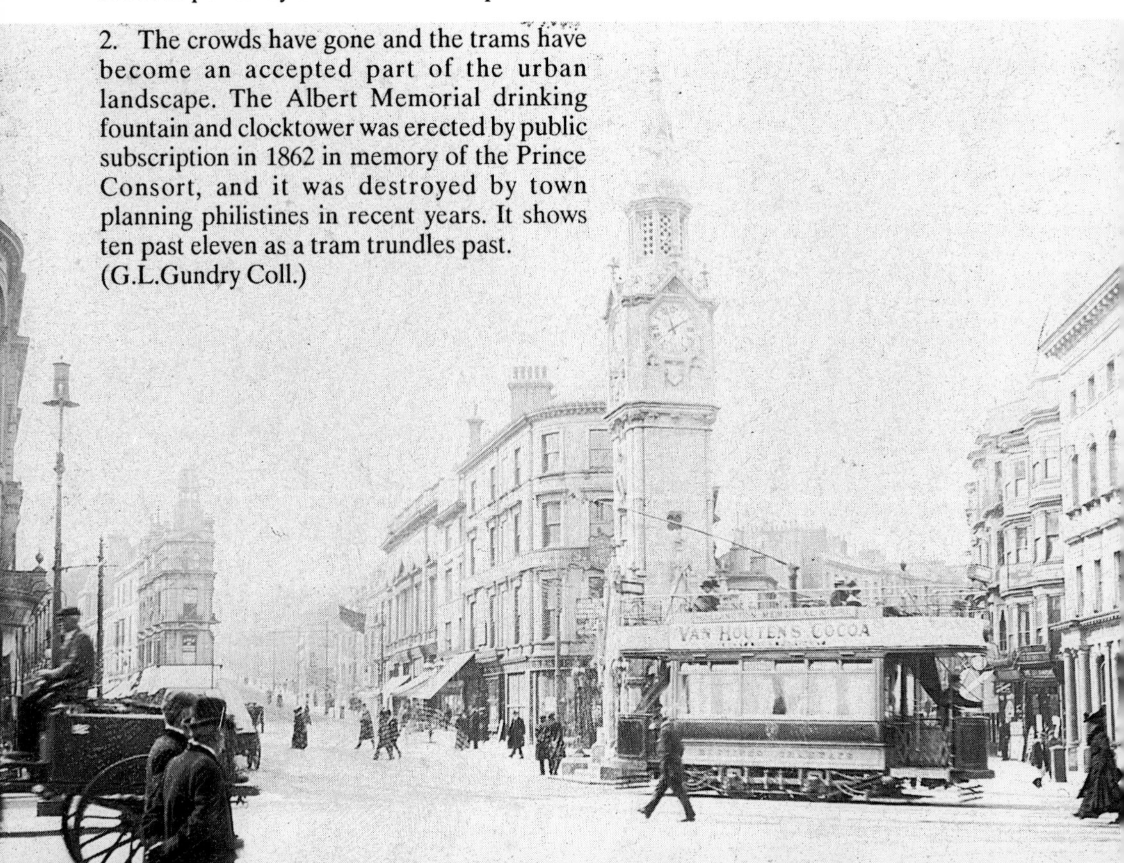

2. The crowds have gone and the trams have become an accepted part of the urban landscape. The Albert Memorial drinking fountain and clocktower was erected by public subscription in 1862 in memory of the Prince Consort, and it was destroyed by town planning philistines in recent years. It shows ten past eleven as a tram trundles past. (G.L.Gundry Coll.)

3. A fine day, although perhaps not that warm as the smoke from the chimneys of H.Rose, Family Grocer indicates. Car 8 passes the cricket ground in Queen's Road. The rest of the town goes about its business, but there's still time for a lad to stop and stare in the middle of the road. (G.L.Gundry Coll.)

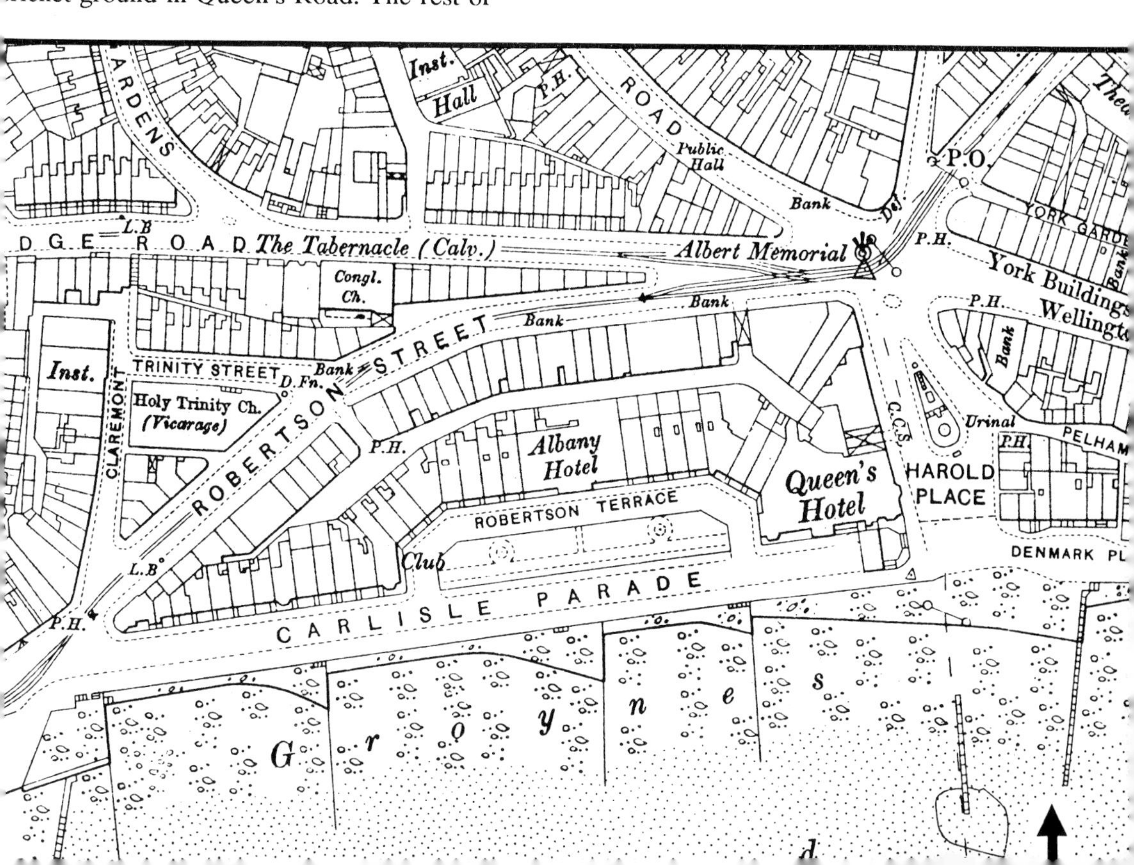

4. Queen's Road again with St. Andrew's Church in the background. Car 27, with a full top deck, passes a group of ladies who seem to be in a bit of a hurry. The young man by the railings has probably been employed to lug around the wicker baskets stacked at the house front; he takes a well earned rest to gaze at the photographer. (D.C.Padgham Coll.)

5. The progress of the official Board of Trade inspection in Queen's Road is watched with interest. Readers of the "History of Mr. Polly" by H.G.Wells will immediately recognise this by-gone world of small shopkeepers. (G.L.Gundry Coll.)

6. St Andrew's "Arch" carrying the railway to Rye and Ashford frames car 24 on its way to St. Helens. Note the "Cars Stop By Request" legend painted on the elegant traction standard. (R.J.Harley Coll.)

SPECIAL
GARAGE
QUEENS
176
ROAD.

FARM DAIRY.

7. Winter sunshine bathes car 20 as it travels under the viaduct which was built in 1898 to replace a narrow brick arch, 120 ft long. Note that even in those far off days digging holes in the pavement and roadway was becoming a national pastime. (D.C.Padgham Coll.)

8. Alexandra Park is to the left of the tram. A smartly dressed gentleman with a walking cane sits watching the sparse traffic and unaware that the statue behind the hedge seems willing to challenge anyone to a joust.
(D.C.Padgham Coll.)

9. Very carefully does it! A brand new tram glides slowly round the curve into St. Helens Park Road. This novel experience for some of the top deck passengers is mirrored in at least one anxious expression as they all begin the descent into the town. (R.J.Harley Coll.)

10. A proud moment for the trainee driver as he halts his charge outside the Langham Hotel before the turn into Elphinstone Road. No doubt, he resisted the temptation of partaking of a "wee dram" of Special Kilmarnock Whisky as advertised by the neighbouring hostelry. (D.C.Padgham Coll.)

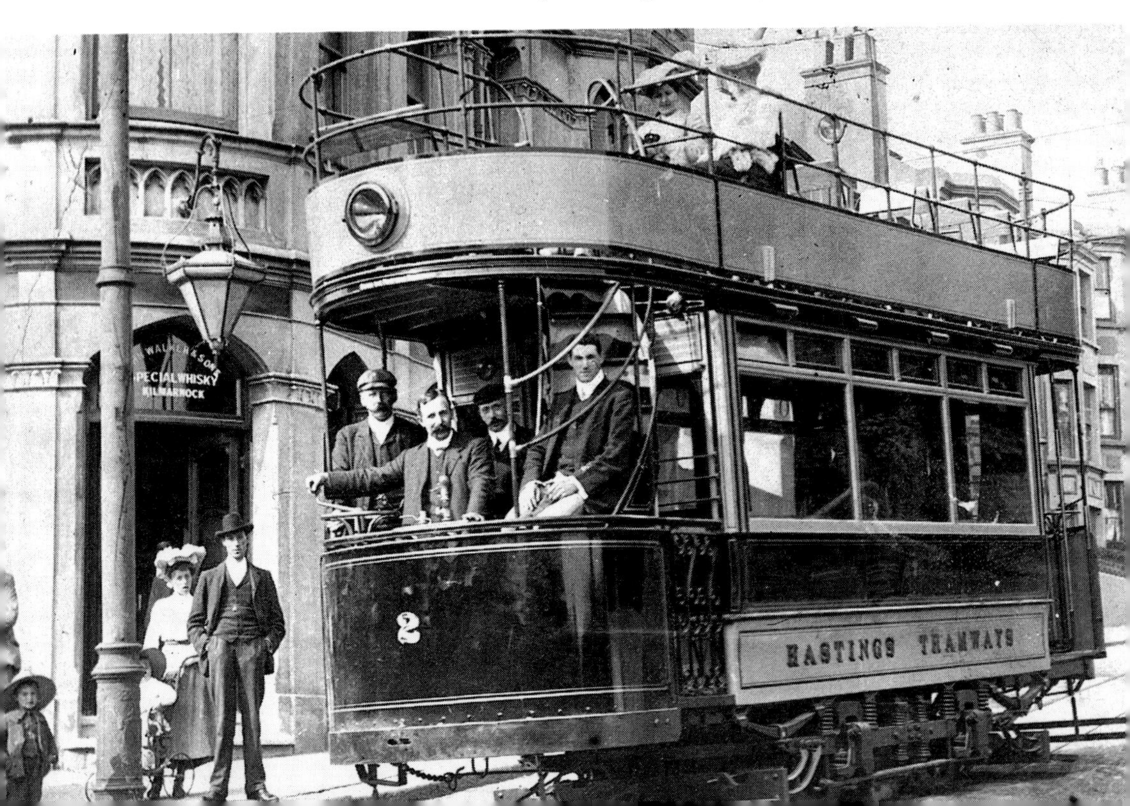

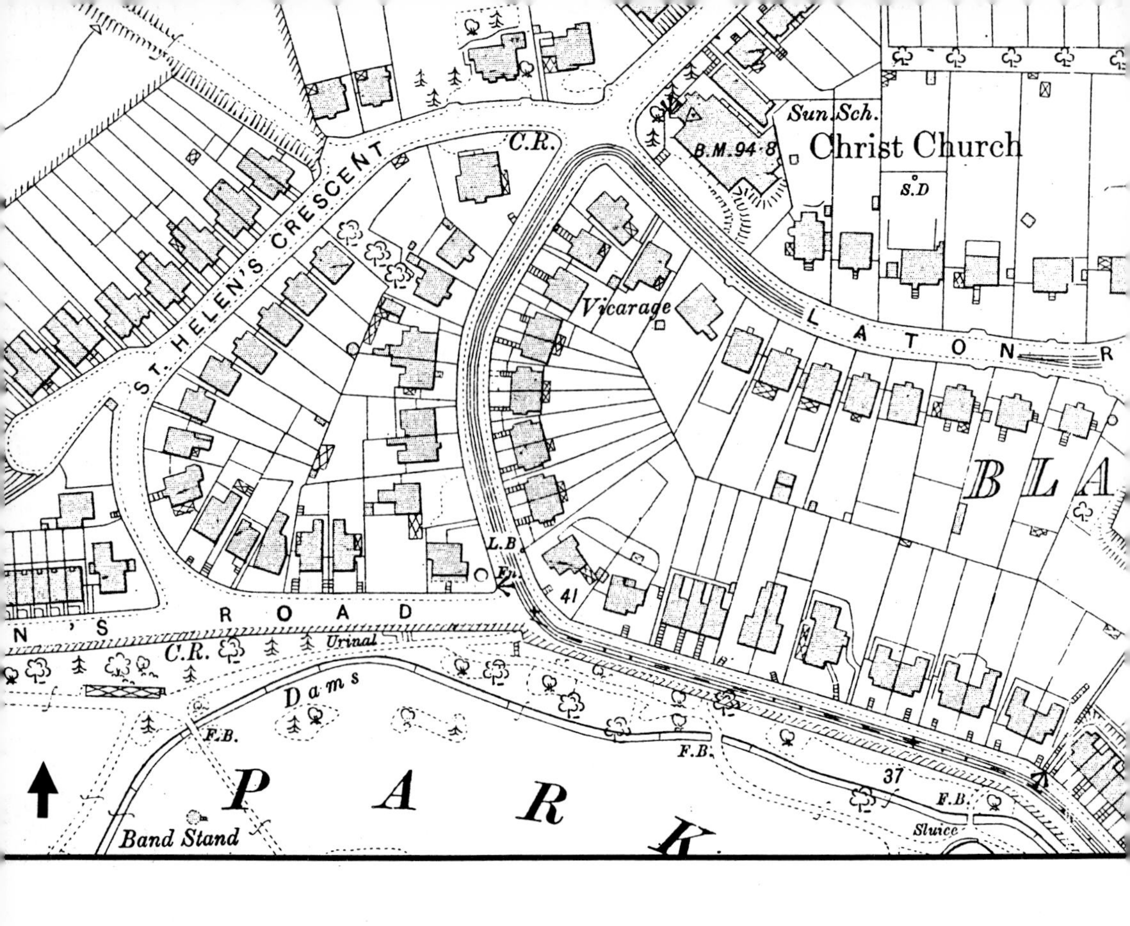

11. A few moments before the previous photo, the same car is caught slowing for the corner. One wonders whether the lady with the two toddlers will shortly patronise the new form of transport. (G.L.Gundry Coll.)

12. Another early view shows car 23 about to turn into Hughenden Road from Elphinstone Road. Although this area was originally known as Pondbay Hill, the tram crews always referred to it as "Bombay Hill." (G.L.Gundry Coll.)

13. Tracklaying is well advanced in Mount Pleasant Road opposite Calvert Road. The local children are interested in the photographer, but the little girl in the foreground is more intent on examining the granite setts. (G.L.Gundry Coll.)

14. The first car on Priory Road, 15th July 1905, with the usual crowd of curious locals viewing its progress; the top deck was probably full of company big-wigs eager to inspect their investment. (D.C.Padgham Coll.)

15. We move on to London Road, Ore, and to the Clive Vale Hotel where the breaking up of the road surface has begun in preparation for the tram track. In those days all work was done manually with pick and shovel.
(G.L.Gundry Coll.)

16. A pleasantly rustic looking Christ Church, Ore, plays host to one of the new circular route trams. Already this excursion was popular with holiday visitors as well as providing much needed transport for the hamlets along the ridge. (G.L.Gundry Coll.)

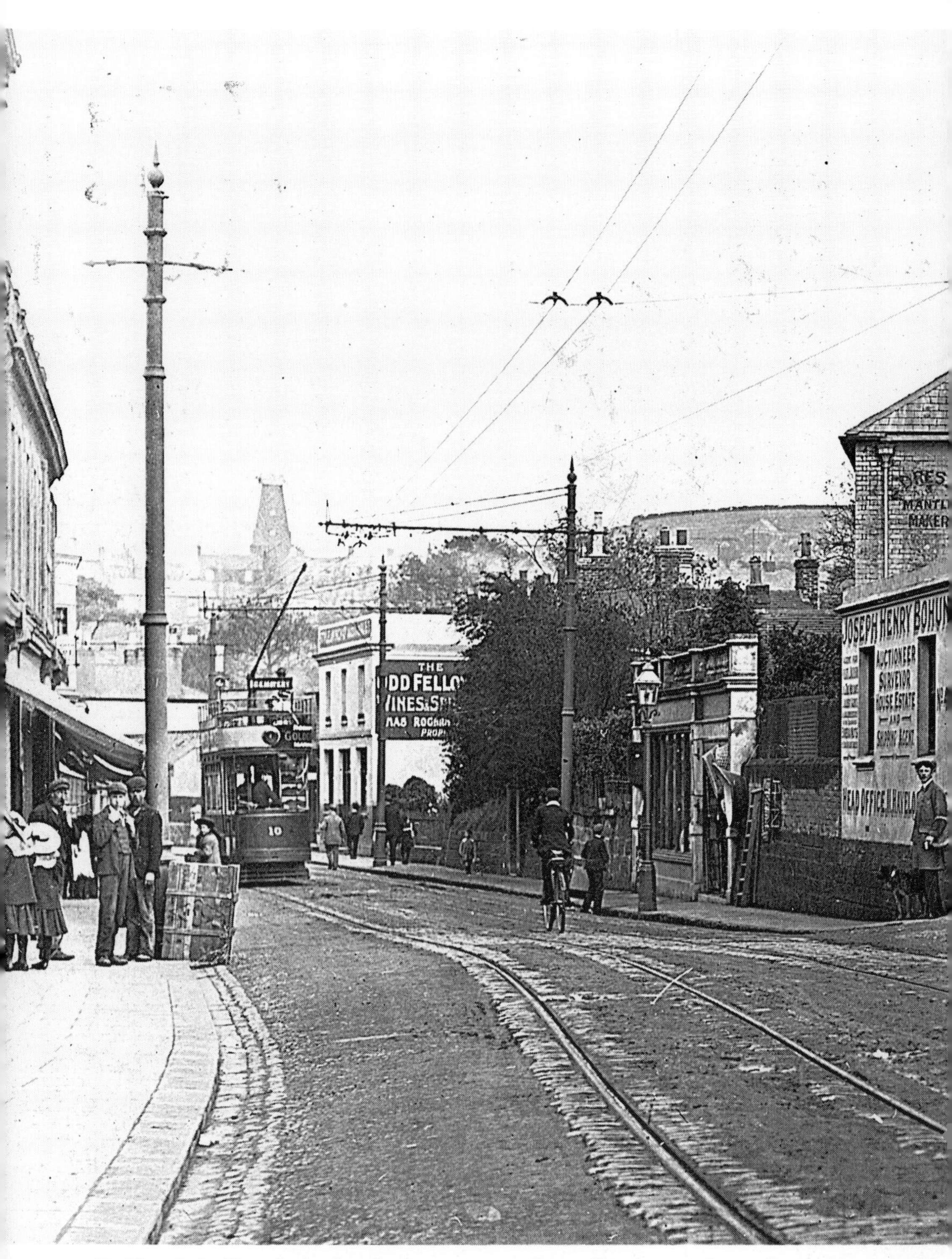

17. The windmill on the horizon looks over car 10 in Old London Road, Ore. The points in the foreground lead onto the tram route down Saxon Road; note the cyclist making sure his wheels are not caught in the rails of the trailing crossover. (G.L.Gundry Coll.)

411

18. The line from Ore to Old Town passed along Harold Road. Car 7 approaches the camera underneath the neat overhead with bracket arms adorned with wrought iron scroll work. (G.L.Gundry Coll.)

19. A fine summer's day, 21st. August 1905, the first day of service along Harold Road. The driver of car 6 has yet to receive his uniform, but he nevertheless is smartly turned out. (G.L.Gundry Coll.)

20. The terminus at Market Cross was the transfer point to the horse bus seen here. A group of ladies are next to the waiting shelter; the conductor waits for the photographer to finish before giving the starting bell for the climb back to Ore. (G.L.Gundry Coll.)

21. The trolley has already been turned by the conductor on the top deck as the driver poses by his car. A little boy in the shadows to the motorman's left no doubt wishes he had a penny for a ride. (R.J.Harley Coll.)

22. The one that got away! The trams never made it down the Old Town High Street, but the trolleybuses managed an unusual service. The narrow road was worked originally on a traffic flow arrangement so that no two buses were allowed to pass on this section. Therefore, the overhead included three wires with the centre wire positive and the other two negative. Single deck Guy trolleybus 40 heads towards St. Helens. (D.Waters Coll.)

23. The experts will tell you that Hastings never had horse trams...partly correct! This view shows an ex-LCC horse car in use as a tea shack for the workers constructing the harbour in the late 1890s. (G.L.Gundry Coll.)

24. Back to Old London Road, Ore, car 64 is negotiating the interlaced track in this late 1920s scene. Above the driver is the service number 6. (D.C.Padgham Coll.)

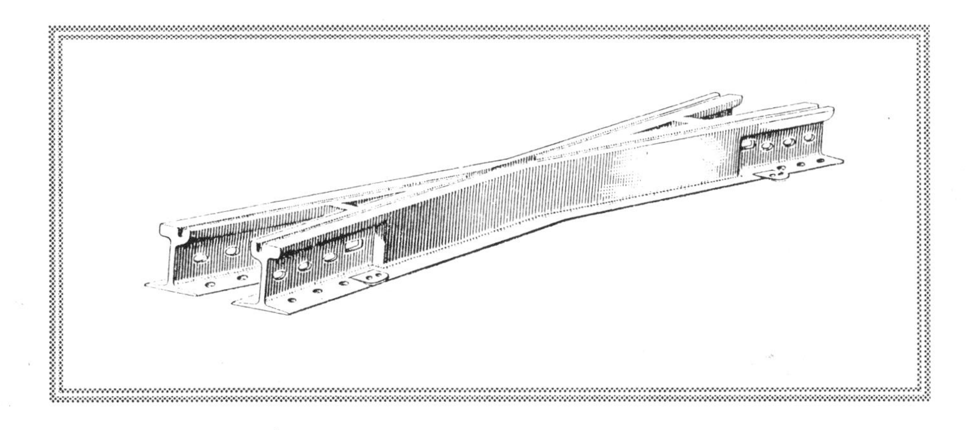

25. Out into the country and car 9 pauses opposite Fairlight Hall, Ore. The date is 31st July 1905, the first day of service. (R.J.Harley Coll.)

26. A tram on a trial trip round Ivyhouse Lane corner. The passengers on the top deck have a good view over the hedgerows as they head through the Wealden countryside. (D.C.Padgham Coll.)

27. The cemetery gates at St. Helens is the setting for car 2 which lays over at the terminus. Behind is the rustic shelter which gave passengers welcome protection from winter gales across the ridge. (G.L.Gundry Coll.)

28. George Gundry was on holiday in 1921 when he took this photo of car 42 at St. Helens. One of the destination boards can be glimpsed propped up against the railings at the top of the staircase above the headlight.
(G.L.Gundry)

Mm 8934

Magdalen Road to Memorial	1d	Park Gates to Memorial
PARK GATES		SPA
SPA		Mt Pleasant Schools
Mt Pleasant Schools		Christ Church Ore
Halton Place		Winchelsea Road
Christ Church Ore		CEMETERY
CEMETERY		Hillside Road
Hillside Road		Harrow Inn
Harrow Inn		Willows
Willows		Upper Church Rd
Upper Church Rd		SILVER-HILL
HOLLINGTON		SILVER-HILL
SILVER-HILL		St. Paul's Road
St. Paul's Road		New Road (Bohemia Road)
Christ Church Ore		GITHA ROAD
GITHA ROAD		HIGH STREET
PARCEL		DOG

Hastings Tramways Company.
Issued subject to Company's Bye-laws and Regulations. Not Transferable.

Williamsc ... ter, Ashton

→

29. Towser stands rigidly on guard as tram's best friend in this posed shot at St. Helens. Ironically dogs were not allowed on the cars. One hopes that the driver is not about to leave with the trolley pole in the wrong direction, as this might result in instant dismissal.

HOLLINGTON
CHIVERS'
JAMS
CHIVERS
JELLIES
29

30. Leafy lanes formed part of the circular route and added to the attractions for summer visitors doing the tour of the circular route. Car 13 trundles through this tranquil picture of a pre- motor age. (G.L.Gundry Coll.)

31. The smock mill at Baldslow stands as a reminder of a centuries old tradition in rural life. The tram is a newcomer on the scene, however, the two forms of power, wind and electricity seem to harmonise well. (D.C.Padgham Coll.)

rk Farm
G.P
B.P
B.S
R.H
F.W
Def.
Inn
3 ft. F.F.
NORTH ROAD
TRAMWAY
3 ft. R.H.
Windmill
(Corn)
2 ft. F.F.
P.O
3 ft. F.W.
436
3 ft. R.H.
BALDSLOW
Quarries

1928 map

32. The village post office was (and still is) a centre of local life. At Baldslow the post office had a tram stop outside and car 14 is just leaving in the direction of the Harrow Inn. (D.C.Padgham Coll.)

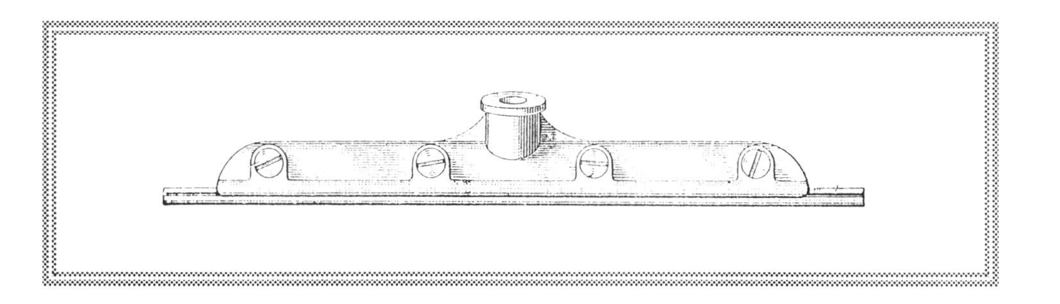

33. A tram waits at the post office Baldslow for a car coming in the opposite direction. Athough many passing loops were not in line of sight, there were no signals. In theory strict adherence to the timetable avoided any embarrassing, or possibly dangerous moments of two cars meeting on the same track. (G.L.Gundry Coll.)

34. Impecunious art students would often ride up from the town to study and sketch at the bridge carrying the tram route over the Sedlescombe Road. The structure would not look out of place in a work by the great English watercolourist John Sell Cotman. Needless to say, road improvements in modern times have resulted in the bridge being replaced by a flyover of no artistic merit. (G.L.Gundry Coll.)

35. Heading south towards town, the route along Sedlescombe Road North was still very rural. Tramways in country lanes were a rarity in Britain, but as can be seen from this early spring view, the tram tracks were clear of competing traffic. (G.L.Gundry Coll.)

36. In tram days urban development on the circular route resumed at Silverhill. In this picture of track construction, the tie bars to keep the rails to gauge can be clearly seen. (D.C.Padgham Coll.)

37. Silverhill was a junction with lines to Hollington and the depot in Beaufort Road. Here a northbound circular route car loads at the tree shaded island, whilst car 35 comes off the Hollington route towards town. Behind, car 4 is about to reverse using the crossover at the bottom of Battle Road. (G.L.Gundry Coll.)

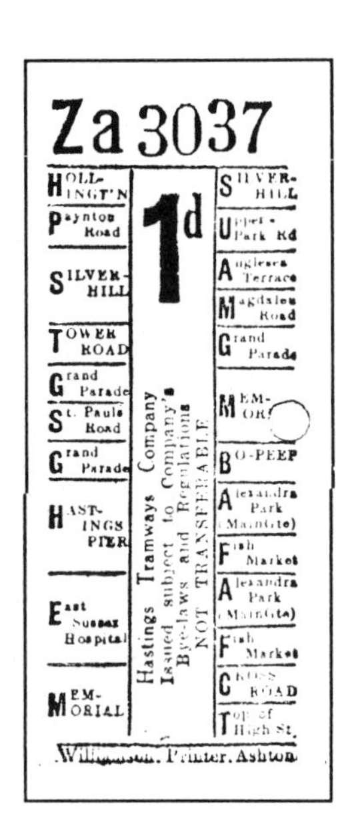

Za 3037

1d

Hastings Tramways Company
Issued subject to Company's
Bye-laws and Regulations
NOT TRANSFERABLE

HOLLINGT'N	SILVERHILL
Paynton Road	Upper Park Rd
SILVERHILL	Anglesea Terrace
TOWER ROAD	Magdalen Road
Grand Parade	Grand Parade
St. Pauls Road	MEMOR[illegible]
Grand Parade	BO-PEEP
HASTINGS PIER	Alexandra Park (MainGte)
East Sussex Hospital	Fish Market
MEMORIAL	Alexandra Park (MainGte)
	Fish Market
	CROSS ROAD
	Top of High St.

Williamson, Printer, Ashton

38. Relief crews wait by car 7 at the island in Silverhill. They had probably walked up from the depot. (G.L.Gundry Coll.)

39. Summer 1906 and car 14 halts at Silverhill. Note the lattice gate across the motorman's platform and the saddler's shop, which provided for the other form of road transport. (G.L.Gundry Coll.)

Front and back of the same ticket.

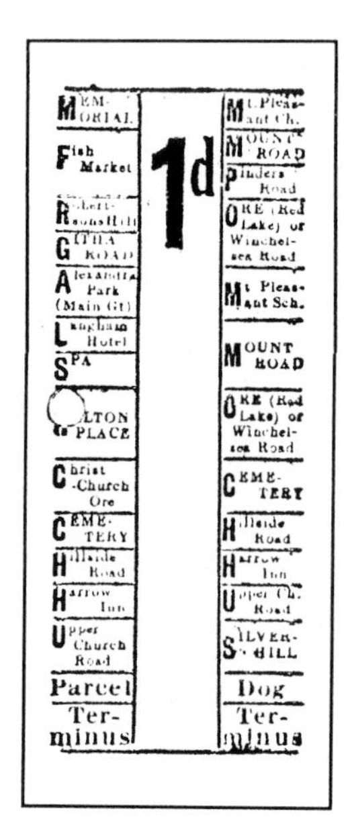

1d

MEMORIAL	Mt. Pleasant Ch.
Fish Market	MOUNT ROAD
Robertsons Hill	Pinders Road
GITHA ROAD	ORE (Red Lake) or Winchelsea Road
Alexandra Park (Main Gt)	Mt Pleasant Sch.
Langham Hotel	MOUNT ROAD
SPA	ORE (Red Lake) or Winchelsea Road
[illegible]LTON PLACE	CEMETERY
Christ-Church Ore	Hillside Road
CEMETERY	Harrow Inn
Hillside Road	Upper Ch. Road
Harrow Inn	SILVERHILL
Upper Church Road	
Parcel	Dog
Terminus	Terminus

40. The connecting tracks to the depot lead off to the right of the picture and it is possible that car 3 may shortly take one to run out of service. (D.C.Padgham Coll.)

41. Battle Road, Hollington is the setting for car 17 on its way to Ore. Notice there is no pavement on the right hand side and that the poles for the bracket arms are actually planted in the road. (G.L.Gundry Coll.)

42. The end of the line, Hollington. An old gentleman looks on suspiciously as the driver and conductor have their photos taken. (D.C.Padgham Coll.)

43. The little girl in the picture turns her head, not looking too happy with the gent in the bowler restraining her hoop, which was a favourite children's plaything in Edwardian times. The motorman seemingly is above all this and he poses stiffly ready for the right of way from Hollington terminus.
(D.C.Padgham Coll.)

44. French visitors celebrating the Entente Cordiale were being "entrammed" at Silverhill in this 1908 view. (D.C.Padgham Coll.)

45. Beaufort Road leads to the depot and it was the scene of much activity in July 1905 when the first runs were made. Car 13 has the destination Kewhurst, the original name for Cooden. (G.L.Gundry Coll.)

46. At the depot frantic preparations are being made for the start of operation. New trams are being fitted out and a traction engine hauls in another member of the fleet; as yet there is no overhead power. A mother points out something to her child as a workman approaches with a pole. (D.Waters Coll.)

A 1749

Hastings Tramways Company

TERMINUS	2D	TERMINUS
Memorial		Bopeep
London Road		Bexhill Road Fare Section
Bopeep		De la Warr Rd. Fare Sec.
Bexhill Road Fare Section		Devonshire Place
De la Warr Rd. Fare Sec.		Metropole Hotel
De la Warr Rd. Fare Sec.		No. 1 Fare Sec. Cooden
Devonshire Place		No. 2 Fare Sec. Cooden
No. 1 Fare Sec. Cooden		Cooden Terminus
DOG		PARCEL

Issued subject to Company's Bye-laws and Regulations. NOT TRANSFERABLE.

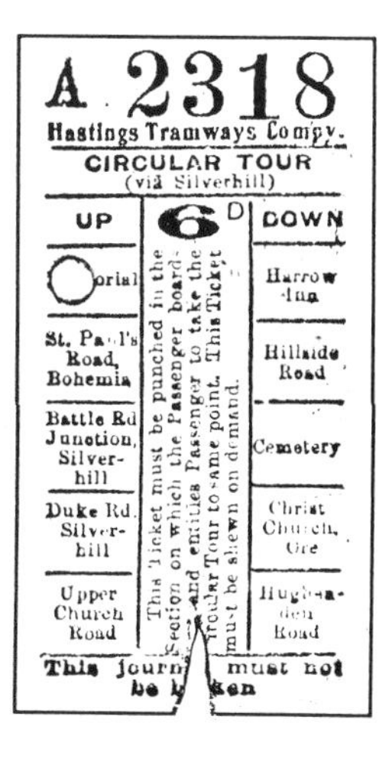

A 2318

Hastings Tramways Compy.

CIRCULAR TOUR

(viâ Silverhill)

UP	6D	DOWN
[illegible]orial		Harrow Inn
St. Paul's Road, Bohemia		Hillside Road
Battle Rd Junction, Silverhill		Cemetery
Duke Rd. Silverhill		Christ Church, Ore
Upper Church Road		Hughenden Road

This Ticket must be punched in the Section on which the Passenger boards and entitles Passenger to take the Circular Tour to same point. This Ticket must be shewn on demand.

This journ[illegible] must not be b[illegible]ken

47. The overhead has now been energised as car 10 sets out for a trial trip from the depot. (R.J.Harley Coll.)

←

48. South of Silverhill, a horse bus edges slowly past the road works signalling its impending doom. Here, outside St. Matthew's Church, the granite setts are being grouted in place either side of the running rails. (D.C.Padgham Coll.)

49. In Bohemia Road a group of girls seem to be having problems hanging on to their hats as a tram sidles into the passing loop by the request stop. (D.C.Padgham Coll.)

Xb 7753

MEMORIAL	4d	CEMETERY
SPA		Hillside Road via Cemetery
Mt Pleas'nt Schools		Harrow Inn via Cemetery
Christ Church Ore		Willows via Cemetery
CEMETERY		DUKE ROAD via Harrow
Hillside Road		SILVERHILL via Harrow
Harrow Inn		St. Paul's Road
Willows		Magdalen Road
Upper Church Rd		MEMORIAL
St. Paul's Road		Mt Pleas'nt Schools via Memorial
PARCEL		FERRY

Hastings Tramways Company.
Issued subject to Company's Bye-laws and Regulations. Not Transferable.

50. Car 9 heads for town past the shops in Bohemia Road. Unusually for that era, a father is seen guiding the infant's push chair at the roadside; the other gentlemen would have been described in the vernacular as "wayside loafers." (G.L.Gundry Coll.)

51. We have now come full circle having arrived at the bottom of Cambridge Road by the Memorial. Cars 21 and 9 pass between a couple of elegant horse drawn conveyances and a more humble delivery cart. As yet there is no evidence of the tram line towards the seafront. (G.L.Gundry Coll.)

52. Passengers board car 27 before it leaves for Silverhill and the Wealden countryside. (D.C.Padgham Coll.)

53. The Memorial was always a much photographed spot, and the author offers no apologies for including a number of tram views at this location. This was very much the central point of the system with a very frequent service. (D.C.Padgham Coll.)

54. In this shot the old horse bus is eking out its days before the inevitable electric shock of the new transport competition. (G.L.Gundry Coll.)

55. Several well dressed pedestrians sweep past car 2 as it halts at the new "Cars Stop Here" sign which has replaced the earlier painted band. (D.C.Padgham Coll.)

56. A last look at a scene now gone for good; note the tracks (lower right) now leading to the seafront and Bexhill. On the hill in the background the remains of the castle bear witness to more violent times.
(G.L.Gundry Coll.)

2. SEAFRONT SERVICE

57. The driver peers round, the final passengers clamber aboard and then we're off on the long run to Cooden Beach in the summer sunshine of the late 1920s. Note the supply cables to the overhead wires. (C.Carter)

58. Robertson Street was originally laid out with the Dolter stud contact system. The studs can be seen in the centre of the single tram track. (G.L.Gundry Coll.)

59. The town's stud trams achieved a certain notoriety and a local publisher produced this card of the fireworks display generated under a car as the 12 ft. long skate bumped its way across the tops of the studs. (G.L.Gundry Coll.)

60. An animated scene on the corner of Robertson Street and the seafront. A policeman wanders along the tram tracks with the Dolter studs clearly visible.
(G.L.Gundry Coll.)

61. White Rock and Robertson Street, as car 48 with the trolley hooked down, sways round the curve. (R.J.Harley Coll.)

62. Car 48 on a return journey, this time the rear destination indicator shows Bexhill and not West Marina which was the end of the Dolter section. The double track tramway was laid against the kerb along the front resulting in many breaches of the rule of the road. The horse and trap in this picture passes to the right of the tram, but in those days common sense prevailed and road users were considerate of one another. (G.L.Gundry Coll.)

63. Looking westwards along the front, a man with a sandwich board tries to drum up business for St. Clement's Caves as a fully laden tram pauses at the stop. (D.C.Padgham Coll.)

65. Past the bandstand car 50 is on a trial trip and halts for the official photograph. Alongside are deckchairs sheeted over and awaiting better weather. (C.Carter)

←

64. The wire brush suspended from the rear fender of car 60 was fitted with electrical contacts to a bell on the tram; its purpose was to detect live studs. When the bell sounded the motorman stopped the car and either he or the conductor gave the offending stud a hefty whack with a rubber headed hammer or a wooden mallet. Then progress would be resumed with no further danger to man or beast. (G.L.Gundry Coll.)

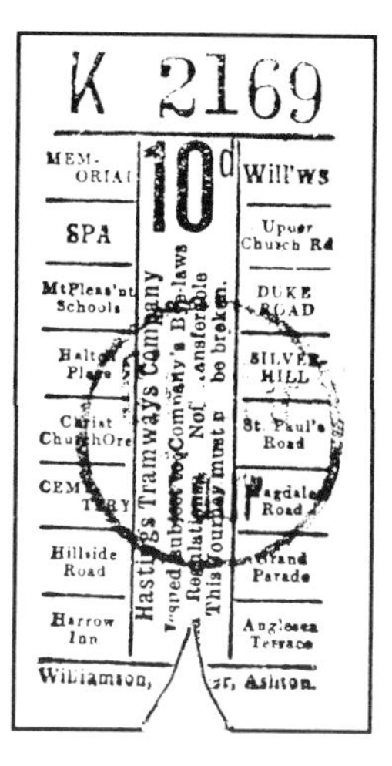

K 2169

10d

Hastings Tramways Company
Issued subject to Company's Bye-laws
Regulations. Not transferable
This journey must not be broken.

MEM-ORIAL	Will'ws
SPA	Upper Church Rd
MtPleas'nt Schools	DUKE ROAD
Halton Place	SILVER HILL
Christ ChurchOre	St Paul's Road
CEMETERY	Magdalen Road
Hillside Road	Grand Parade
Harrow Inn	Anglesea Terrace

Williamson, Printer, Ashton.

66. The elegant facades reflect the winter sunshine along White Rock Parade. Out of season the top deck of car 41 provides a bracing, chilly ride for a few hardy souls. (G.L.Gundry Coll.)

68. In 1920 overhead wires and these stylish bracket arms were erected along the front. Car 17 is testing the overhead which appears to need retensioning a little.
(D.C.Padgham Coll.)

←

67. The White Rock Pavilion was officially opened on 6th April 1927 by HRH The Prince of Wales, later King Edward VIII. The "people's prince" spent the whole day in the town, and the visit is still regarded with much affection. Here the noble edifice plays host to the Royal Sanitary Institute Congress. A steam lorry is parked outside as a tram slips past using the new overhead system.
(G.L.Gundry Coll.)

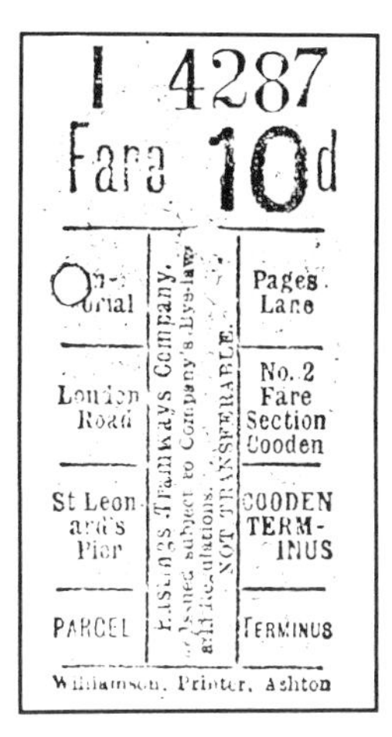

WATNEYS ALE

ISS

69. Hastings Pier is the splendid setting for a summer concert. Heads turn on the tram as the entertainment is about to begin. The Pier gave rise to much tram traffic. (G.L.Gundry Coll.)

70. Steamer trips were popular and a vessel can just be seen by the pier. On the promenade a motor car passes an Ore bound tram running in the opposite direction.
(D.C.Padgham Coll.)

71. We have no evidence to suppose that the Austrian Emperor Franz Josef was strolling along incognito, when the photographer for Louis Levy postcards snapped him inspecting a bicycle opposite Warrior Square, St. Leonards. The invalid carriages are waiting for custom as car 44 grinds along with a full load.
(R.J.Harley Coll.)

WEST MARINA
GRAND PARADE ST LEONARDS ON SEA.

St Leonards from London Road.

72. Car 42 slows for the junction with the London Road tramway. (R.J.Harley Coll.)

74. Looking north along London Road, a tram is ready to depart for Silverhill, with the trolley is on a wire over the track adjacent to the tram. (G.L.Gundry Coll.)

73. In the distance a tram comes off the single track section in front of the South Colonnade, St. Leonards. Those students of tramway overhead should find much of interest in the matching of the new seafront wiring with the older curves into London Road. (G.L.Gundry Coll.)

D 4707
HASTINGS
Tramways Company.

PARCEL	5d	TERMINUS
Memorial		Devonshire
London Road	subject to Bye laws and ... of the Company. NOT TRANSFERABLE.	Metropole Hotel
London Road		No. 1 Fare Section Cooden
Bopeep		No. 2 Fare Section Cooden
Bexhill Rd. Fare Sec.		Cooden Terminus

Punch & Ticket Co., Ld., London

75. The trolley has been turned; note the steep gradient which the tram will shortly have to tackle on its return. (G.L.Gundry Coll.)

76. The Channel is in the background as a group of workmen sets about constructing the London Road tramway. Such work was always labour intensive as there were few mechanical aids. (D.C.Padgham Coll.)

77. The two churches in London Road dwarf a tram making the descent to the seafront. (D.C.Padgham Coll.)

TOWER HO
WINE & SPIRIT ST
SALOON BAR
CARRIAGES

WEST MARINA
MEMORIAL

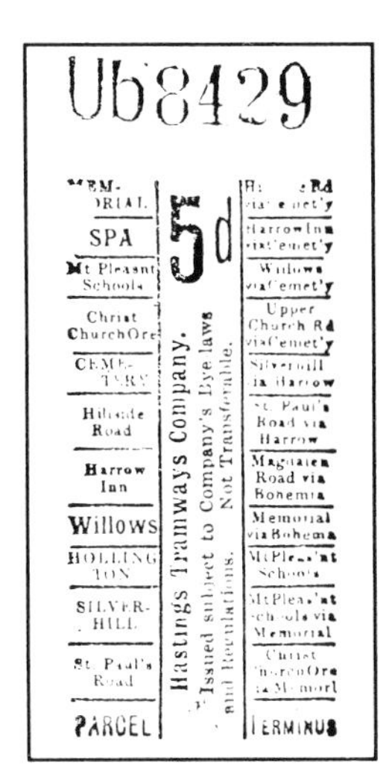

78. The destination on car 31 says Grand Parade as the car prepares to pass the baker's delivery trap. Perhaps the occupant had just slipped into the saloon bar of the Tower Hotel. (R.J.Harley Coll.)

79. Our journey continues along the seafront; two trams set down passengers, some of whom are transferring to the Silverhill car waiting out of shot in London Road. (R.J.Harley Coll.)

80. A motor car, with the early registration A 8478, is parked on St. Leonards Parade as the only other mechanised transport aside from the two trams. (R.J.Harley Coll.)

81. Some minor road works are going on as car 45 enters the curve onto the single track by the Colonnade. (G.L.Gundry Coll.)

82. Car 60 has just cleared the single track and its live stud detecting wire brush trails obediently behind. (G.L.Gundry Coll.)

83. One wonders why all the fuss was made about intrusive overhead wires when the neat final arrangement pictured here could have been erected years earlier, thus saving much expense on Dolter studs and petrol electric trams. (D.C.Padgham Coll.)

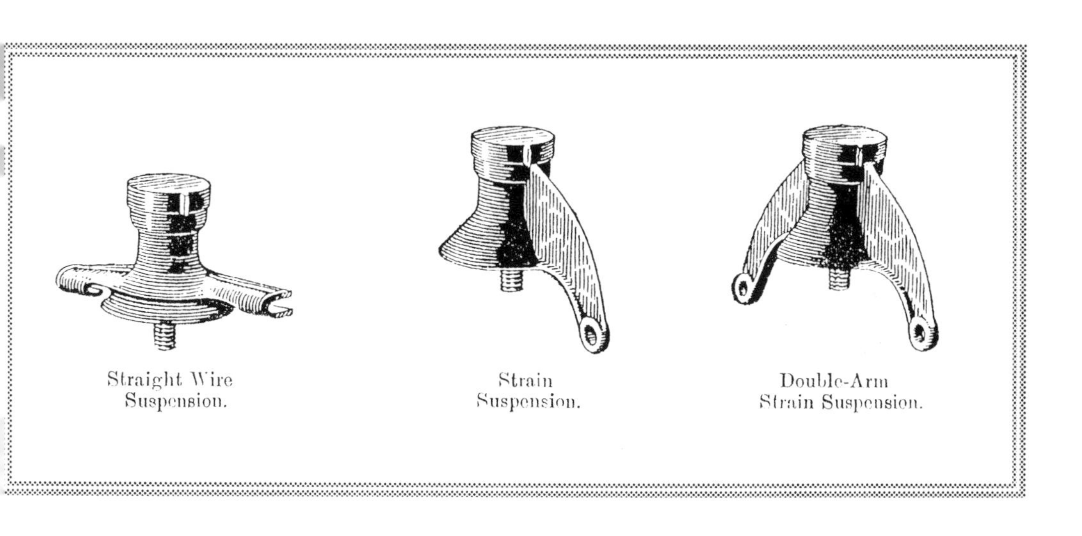

BEXHILL
RLOUR.
The Hastings Invasion.
No1. March 17th 1909. Judges.

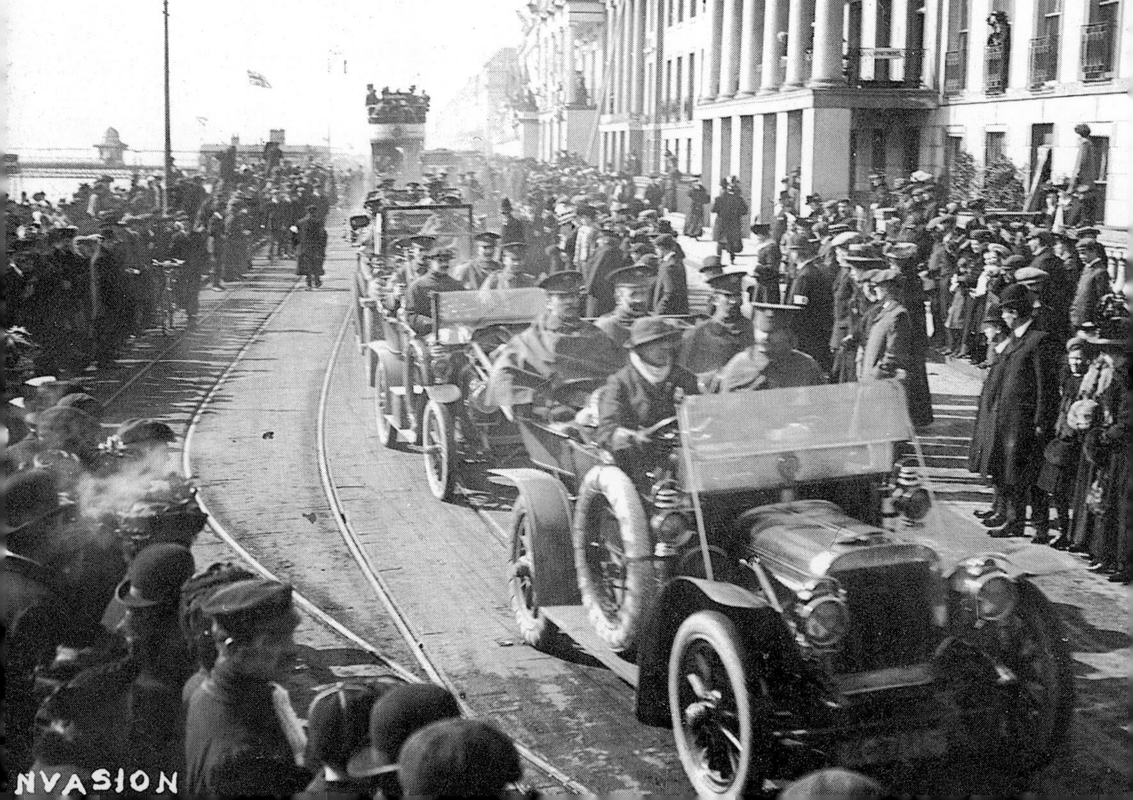
NVASION

84. Subsequent to THE invasion in 1066, a later military expedition reached Hastings on 17th March 1909. This was to test the practicality of a motorised mobilisation of troops. Here we see the assembled masses blissfully unaware of the Hastings Tramways own secret weapon, a live Dolter stud! Happily there were no reports of soldiers suffering exploding boots or dancing 500 volt inspired jigs along the front! (G.L.Gundry Coll.)

86. The motorman on car 46 is no doubt looking forward to the end of the journey as he approaches West Marina. (R.J.Harley Coll.)

85. One final view of the motorised cavalcade, with St. Leonards Pier in the background. Bearing in mind the novelty of the occasion, the soldiers look reasonably relaxed after their dusty ride from the capital. (G.L.Gundry Coll.)

87. One final view at St. Leonards Marina as a couple of ladies prepare to board Hastings bound car 45. (G.L.Gundry Coll.)

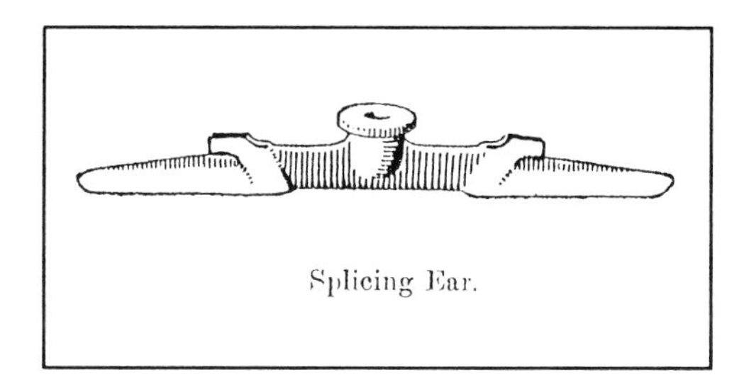

←

88. The tracks at West Marina curve inland and car 44 stands opposite a horse drawn oil delivery wagon. Note the road patching gang on the left of the picture who seem to have done some work already next to the tram rails. (D.C.Padgham Coll.)

89. In the summer of 1951 trams returned to the seafront, albeit in miniature form. In this rare view open and closed narrow gauge cars pass at a loop. The tramway was operated by Claude Lane, who later set up down the coast at The Crumbles near Eastbourne. The current descendants of these miniatures now operate at Seaton in Devon. (D.C.Padgham)

SPECIAL
HASTINGS & BEXHILL
BEXHILL
ROBINS &
BOP
C. WEBBE
HASTINGS
41
rst Tram, Front Line
Hastings & St Leonards 18/12/06
J. Sp
MEMORIAL
HUDS
SUPER
63

90. The trolley of the car behind is on the wire leading to Bexhill, whereas car 41 has its trolley boom stowed as the driver gingerly edges forward drawing power from the studs in the roadway between the rails. (R.J.Harley Coll.)

92. At the changeover point by the Bopeep a Bexhill car waits to depart. The signboard is over the gates to the LBSCR's St. Leonards West Marina station, which closed in 1967. (R.J.Harley Coll.)

91. Car 63 waits to reverse to return to the Memorial. It is standing at the very end of the Dolter stud track and above the car can be seen the conventional overhead wires for the Bexhill and Cooden services. (G.L.Gundry Coll.)

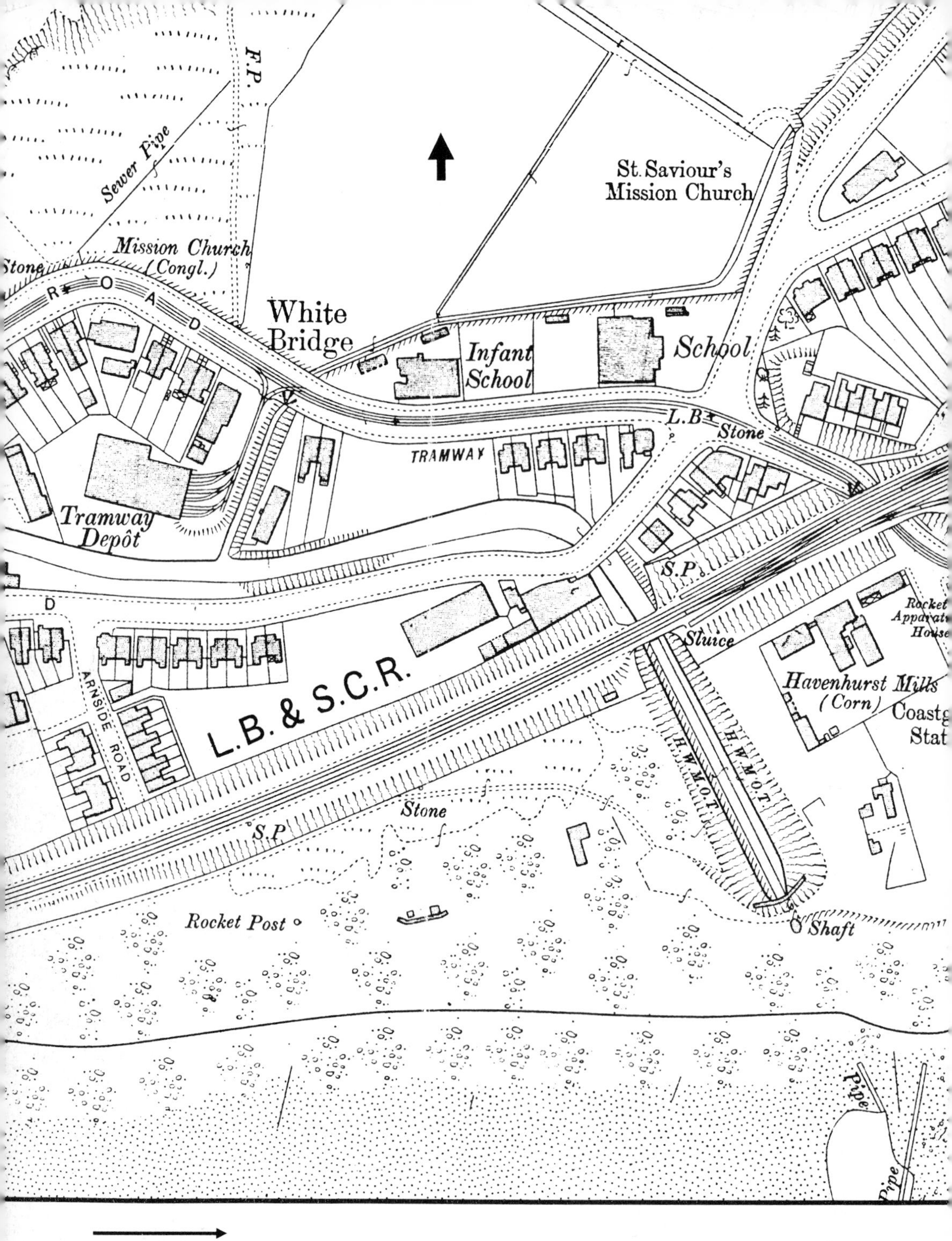

93. Clearances are being checked as car 32 emerges from the shadows underneath the bridge carrying the LBSCR main line from St. Leonards to Eastbourne The railway opened halts at Collington, Glyne Gap and Cooden in 1905 to compete with the trams. Sadly, no photograph was found that included the tram depot that is shown on the map, lower left. (G.L.Gundry Coll.)

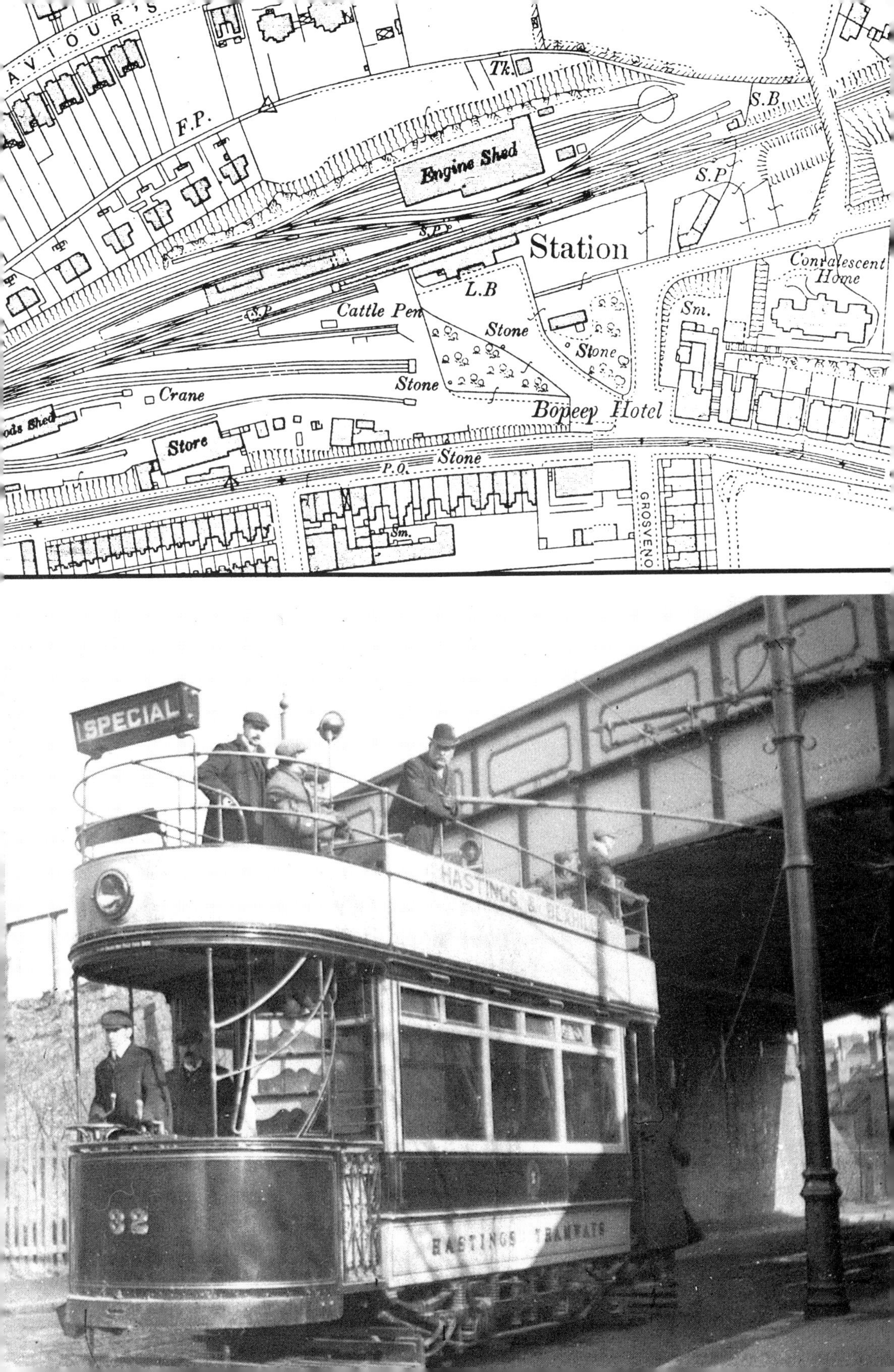

AVIOUR'S
F.P.
Tk.
S.B
Engine Shed
S.P
S.P
Station
Convalescent Home
L.B
Cattle Pen
S.P
Stone
Stone
Sm.
Stone
Crane
Bopeep Hotel
Store
P.O.
Stone
Sm.
GROSVENO
SPECIAL
HASTINGS & BEXHILL
32
HASTINGS TRAMWAYS

94. Full stop on the reserved track across Pebsham Marsh, as the conductor puts the trolley back on the wire. Perhaps the tram had been exceeding the speed limit implied by the notice on the traction standard which instructed drivers only to use series notches on

the controller. At the end of the private right of way there was a corresponding notice saying "Parallel Permitted", and normal speed could be resumed. (D.C.Padgham Coll.)

3. BEXHILL

95. De La Warr Road leads towards Bexhill and in this early 1930s view the tram track is being removed. The old tramway bracket arms were retained and two extra negative wires were added for the trolleybuses. (D.C.Padgham Coll.)

96. Reputedly car 39 was the first tram in Bexhill. Here it is on its historic journey at the corner of Magdalen Road and Sea Road. (G.L.Gundry Coll.)

97. At the same corner as the previous view, car 36 shows local dignitaries and company officials over the new lines. (G.L.Gundry Coll.)

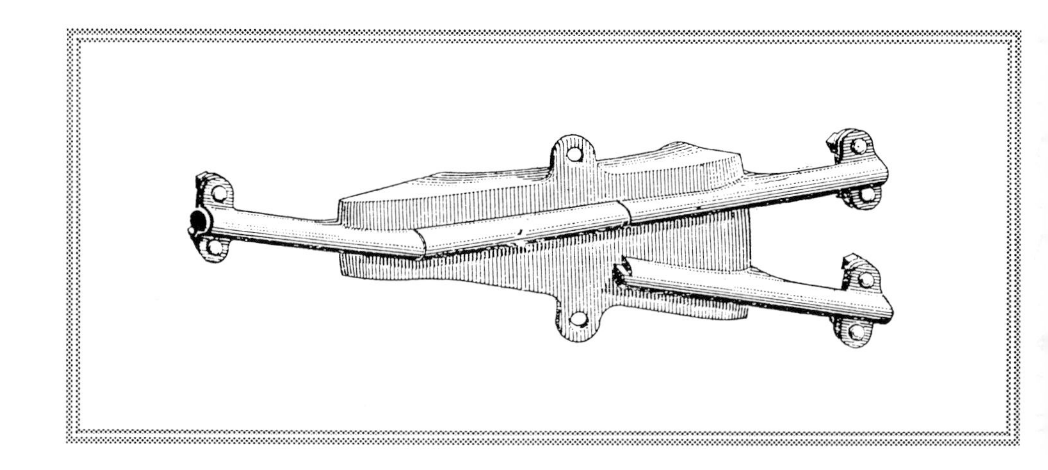

98. Car 55 is outside St. Mary Magdalen Church in Upper Sea Road. The tram is about to cross the bridge over the LBSCR south coast line at Bexhill Central station. (D.C.Padgham Coll.)

UCKH
Bapt. Chap.
CLIFFORD ROAD
CRANFIELD ROAD
UPP
Ward Bdy
C.R.
Club
Institute
R. C. Church
UPPER STATION ROAD
Station
L.B.
ENDWELL ROAD
STATION SQUARE
Hotel
Granville Hotel
Bk.
ST LEONARDS ROAD
ROAD
L.B
Bl.
DEVONSHIRE ROAD
Bk.
P.O.
EVERSLEY ROAD
WILTON ROAD
SEA ROAD
Vicarage
St. Barn
BRASSEY ROAD

99. Devonshire Road is in the fashionable centre of Bexhill and the tramway company enhanced the image by installing an elegant line of centre poles topped by street lamps. (G.L.Gundry Coll.)

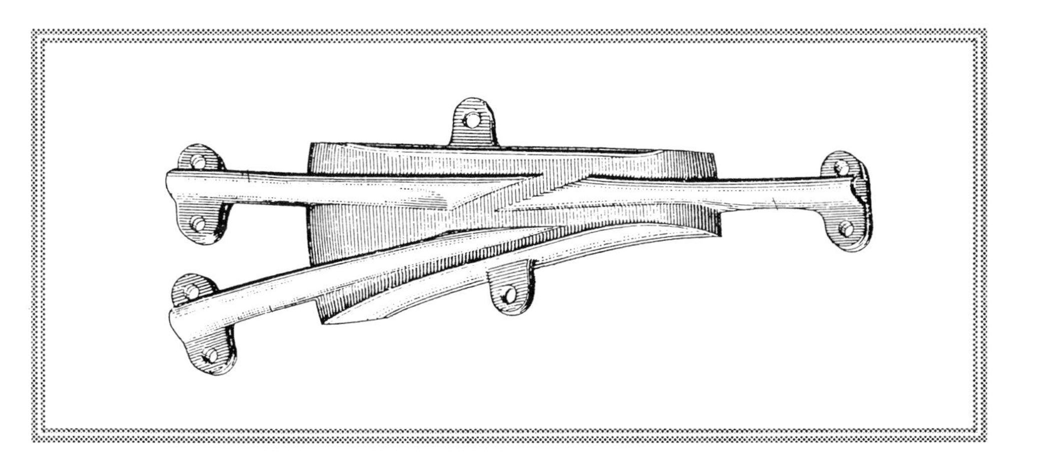

101. Pole painting is taking place in this 1920s view; the lamps had now been repositioned on either side of the traction wires.
(G.L.Gundry Coll.)

←

100. Looking northwards we see car 34 rolling sedately down Devonshire Road. Bexhill was fond of its trams and it was widely held that they gave the town a very modern image.
(G.L.Gundry Coll.)

HASTINGS & BEXHILL

102. A policeman scans the road as he waits at the request stop for a westbound car to Cooden. The white band on the pole carries the words "Cars stop on request". (R.J.Harley Coll.)

103. You can almost hear the wheels of the tram scraping round the right angle bend. Maybe the conductor is looking out for potential customers as his car seems almost empty. (R.J.Harley Coll.)

104. High summer at the Metropole corner on Bexhill Marina sees two trams stopped just beyond the short-working terminal crossover outside the hotel. Car 43 pictured here was subsequently rescued by Dover Transport Museum. (R.J.Harley Coll.)

105. Car 45 is loading passengers and then it will reverse for the journey back to Hastings. The tracks in the foreground lead into Egerton Road. (R.J.Harley Coll.)

106. At the same position as the previous view, car 36 illustrates the splendid condition in which the cars were maintained. Note the enamelled stop sign. (G.L.Gundry Coll.)

107. Few people now realise that Egerton Road once boasted a double track tramway. In contrast to many streets used by the trams which have changed out of all recognition in the motor age, this particular road is now (1993) a quiet backwater with the Bexhill Museum located on the left. (D.C.Padgham Coll.)

4. COODEN

108. Cooden Drive was built for the trams and it crossed open country with cornfields either side of the tramroad. In Winter the service was infrequent and the motorman would sometimes take shelter inside the lower saloon as the car drove itself along this isolated stretch to the terminus. New housing had appeared by the time this photo was taken. (D.C.Padgham Coll.)

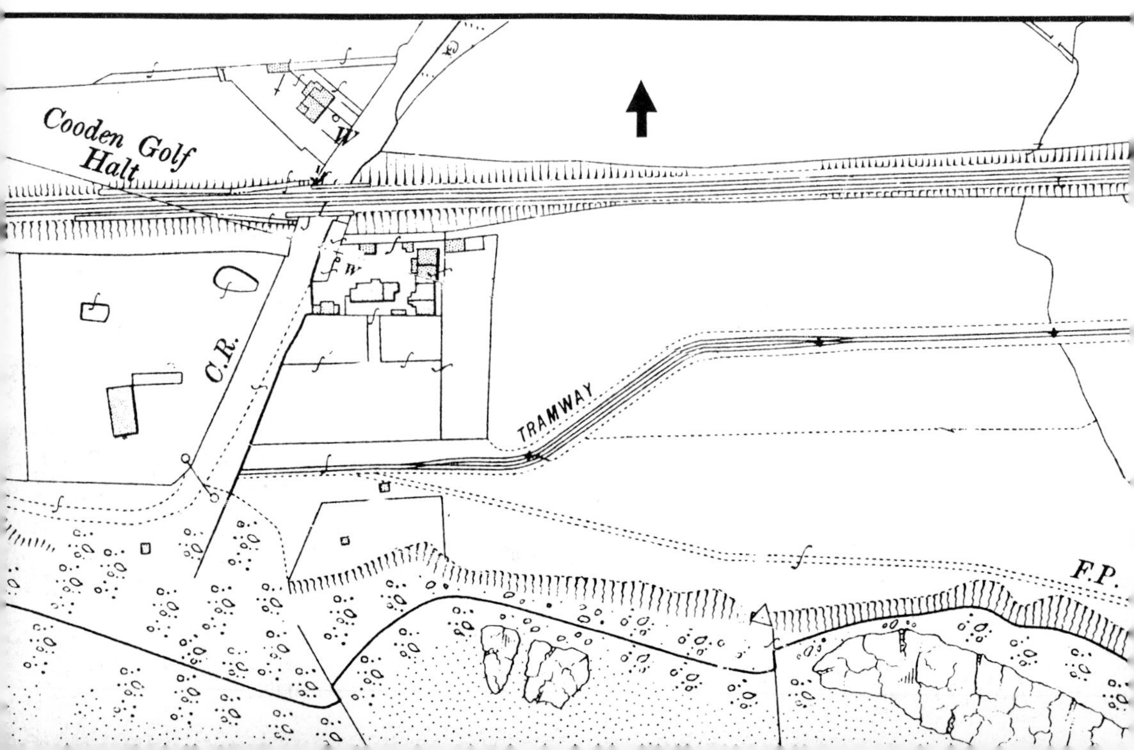

109. Nearing the end of the track, car 45 slows for the final bend at Cooden Beach. (G.L.Gundry)

110. A few coastguard cottages were once the only signs of habitation at what was then termed Kewhurst. The trams opened up the area to an extent and the car here is standing by the passing loop. Amongst the attractions for potential trippers a local guide book noted..."blackberries abound, and the golden gorse gives an ever-welcome splash of colour". (G.L.Gundry Coll.)

111. After the demise of the trams the track remained for some years. One of the replacing trolleybuses is seen here about to pursue a Maidstone and District single deck motor bus back to Bexhill. (G.L.Gundry Coll.)

112. We need to catch our breath after our tram tour of Hastings and what better place than the beach at Cooden. A flag flutters in the warm breeze as a lady in her summer costume glides towards the waiting tramcar; on the shore a fishing boat is beached and this atmosphere of long ago seems very inviting. (G.L.Gundry Coll.)

5. ROLLING STOCK

All the Hastings vehicles were of the traditional British open top, open platform, four wheel variety. The fleet numbered 65 cars; all were manufactured at Preston and ran on 5ft. 6ins./1676mm. wheelbase trucks. They seated 20 in the lower saloon and 22 on the top deck. Livery was originally described as chocolate and yellowish cream, however, other eye witnesses liken the 1920s livery to a claret wine colour and cream. At this distance in time it is difficult to be totally certain. On the waist panel the monogram HT was surrounded by a belt and buckle device and HASTINGS TRAMWAYS was displayed in gold letters on the rocker panel. Only about half the fleet was equipped with the Dolter gear and some of these cars, probably by then around 24 in number, were converted to petrol electric traction. All cars were fitted with trolleys. Cars 41 - 60 were later dual fitted for stud and overhead.

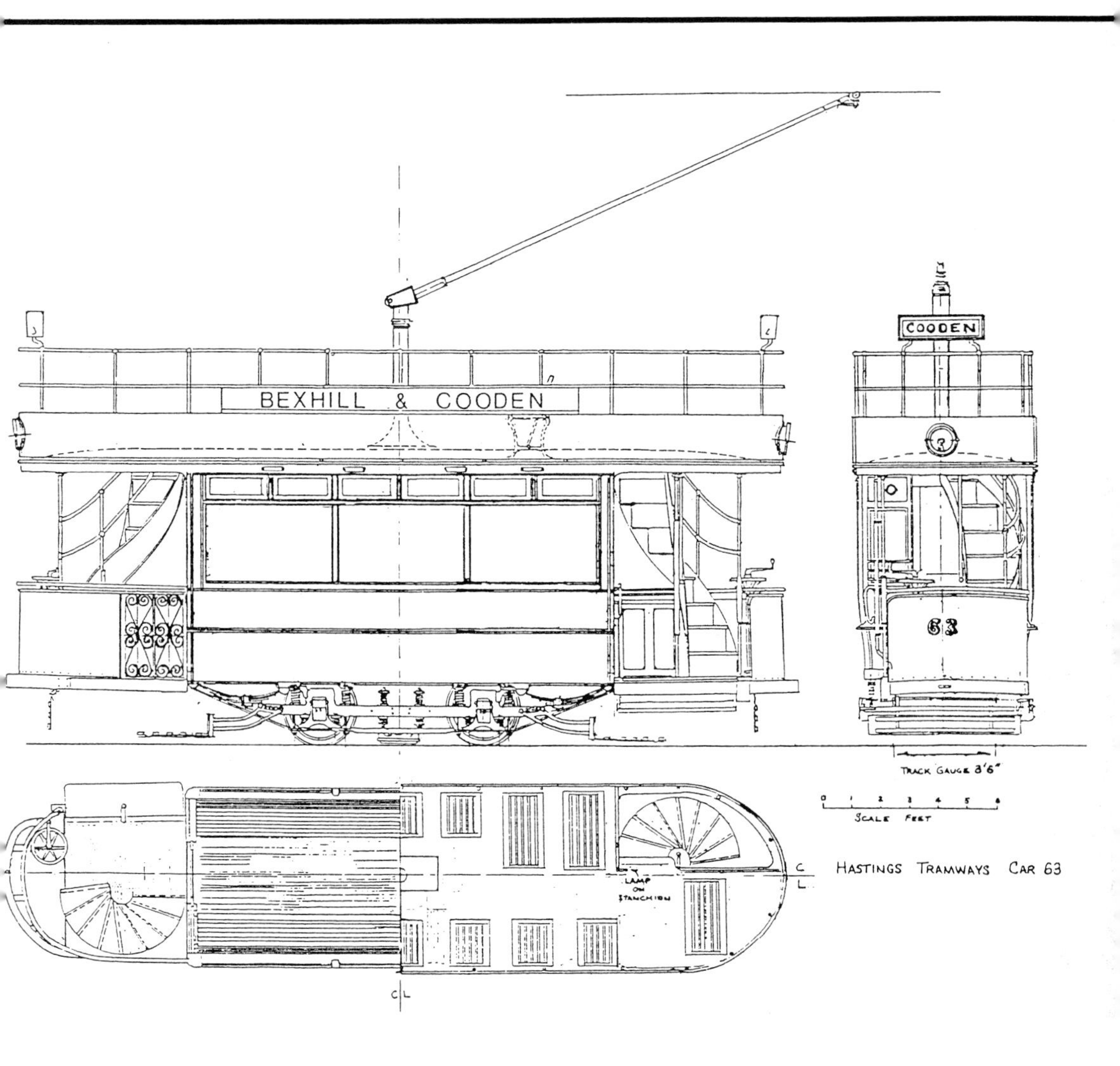

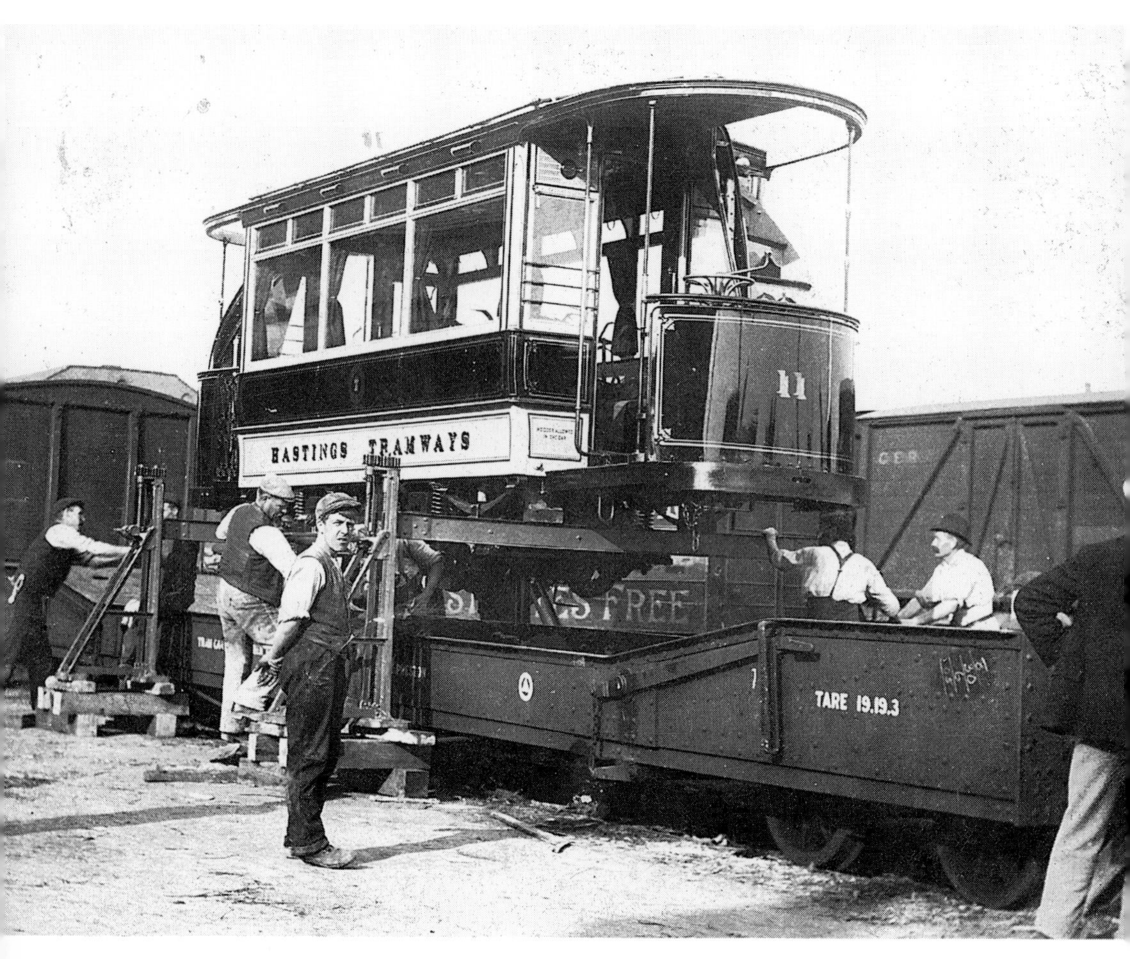

113. A proud moment as the first cars are gently lifted from their railway delivery wagons to await suitable road transport to the nearest tram lines. (D.C.Padgham Coll.)

→

114. In Cambridge Road car 12 is still jacked up ready for the next stage of the delivery. Notice that the upper deck decency boards were secured flat to the car roof and the upper deck seats were stacked in the lower saloon. (D.C.Padgham Coll.)

HASTINGS TRAMWAYS

115. Gently does it as car 11 is eased down temporary rails to the road surface.
(G.L.Gundry Coll.)

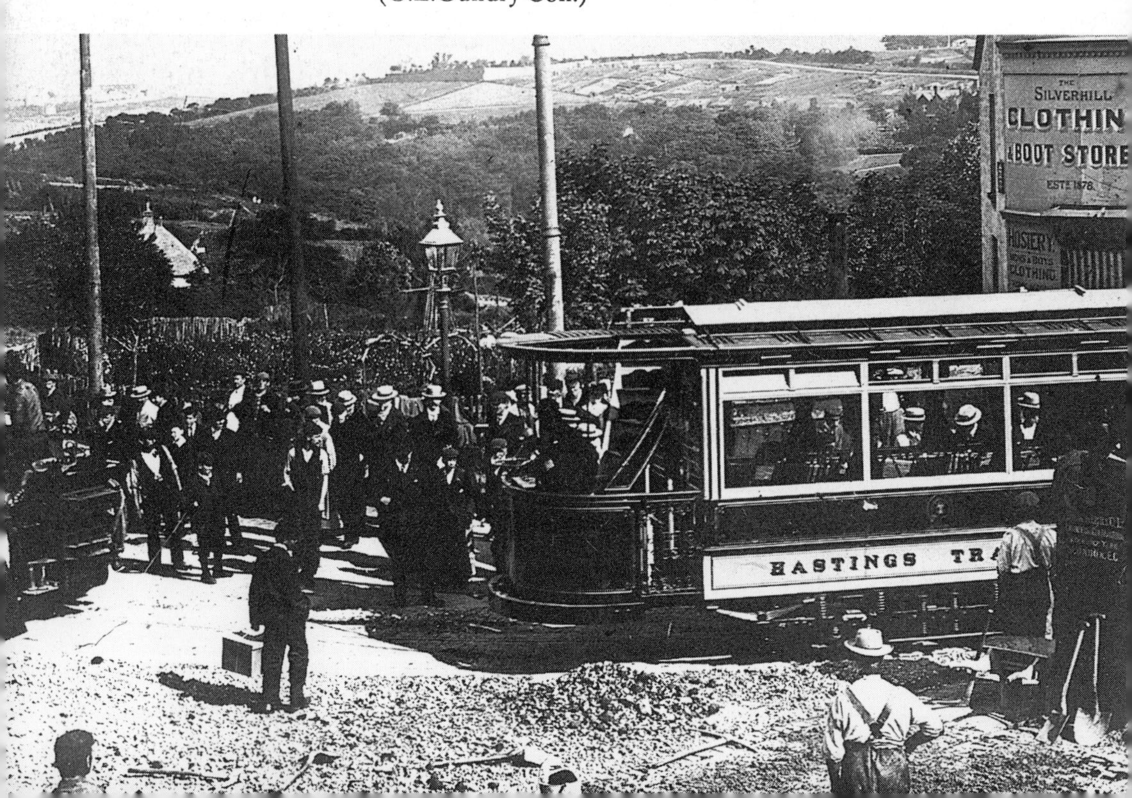

117. In later years the depot contained a tower wagon featured in the background and a car fitted with a snow plough in the winter months. (G.L.Gundry Coll.)

←

116. The trams were then towed by traction engine to the depot at Silverhill. (D.C.Padgham Coll.)

118. A rare picture of a petrol electric car sometime during the First World War. The exhaust pipe can be seen to the right of the conductress and in certain wind conditions exhaust fumes used to waft over the whole car. (D.C.Padgham Coll.)

119. A detailed broadside view of a tram being kitted out for some theatre advertising. You can just make out the two ends of the Dolter skate fitted under the car. (D.C.Padgham Coll.)

120. The tramway power station was constructed in Parker Road, Ore. Here we see the 175 ft. tall chimney which was fabricated from steel plates and erected by Babcock & Willcox. There was a railway siding from the SECR. (G.L.Gundry)

Easebourne Lane, Midhurst, West Sussex. GU29 9AZ
Tel: (0730) 813169 Fax: (0730) 812601

• Write or telephone for our full list of albums •

Other Tramway Albums

by the same author

Brighton's Tramways
Thanet's Tramways
Greenwich and Dartford Tramways

Bus Books

Tillingbourne Bus Story
Eastbourne Bus Story

Other Sussex Books

East Grinstead Then & Now
Betwixt Petersfield and Midhurst
Walking Ashdown Forest
Battle over Sussex 1940
Military Defence of West Sussex
Kent & East Sussex Waterways
Brickmaking in Sussex

Local Middleton Press Railway albums

Orpington to Tonbridge
Redhill to Ashford
Branch Line to Hawkhurst
Branch Line to Tenterden
Branch Lines to Tunbridge Wells
Eastbourne to Hastings